D1289684

BOOKS, CULTURE AND CHARACTER

BOOKS, CULTURE
AND CHARACTER

BY

JOSEPHUS NELSON LARNED

BOOKS FOR LIBRARIES PRESS
FREEPORT, NEW YORK

First Published 1906
Reprinted 1969

STANDARD BOOK NUMBER:
8369-1211-X

LIBRARY OF CONGRESS CATALOG CARD NUMBER:
70-90650

PRINTED IN THE UNITED STATES OF AMERICA

CONTENTS

I

A FAMILIAR TALK ABOUT BOOKS

A FAMILIAR TALK ABOUT BOOKS [1]

I WAS asked to say something to you about books; but when I began to collect my thoughts it seemed to me that the subject on which I really wished to speak is not well defined by the word Books.

If you had been invited to listen to a discourse on baskets, you would naturally ask, " Baskets of what?" The basket, in itself, would seem to be a topic so insignificant that you might reasonably object to the wasting of time on it. It is a thing which has no worth of its own, but borrows all its useful value from the things which are put into it. It belongs

[1] Addressed originally to the students of the Central High School, Buffalo, N. Y.

to a large class of what may be called the conjunctive utensils of mankind — the vessels and vehicles which are good for nothing but to hold together and to carry whatever it may be that men need to convey from one to another or from place to place.

Now, books are utensils of that class quite as distinctly as baskets are. In themselves, as mere fabrications of paper and ink, they are as worthless as empty wickerware. They differ from one another in value and in interest precisely as a basket of fruit differs from a basket of coals, or a basket of garbage from a basket of flowers, — which is the difference of their contents, and that only. '

So it is not, in reality, of books that I wish to speak, but of the contents of books. It may be well for us to think of books in that way, as vessels — vehicles — carriers — because it leads us, I am sure, to more clearly classified ideas of them. It puts them all into one category, to begin with, as carriers in the commerce of mind with mind; which instantly suggests that there are divisions of kind in that commerce, very much as there are divisions of kind in the mercantile traffic of the world; and we proceed naturally to some proper assorting of the mind-matter which books are carriers for. The division we are likely to recognize first is one that separates all which we commonly describe to ourselves as Knowledge, from everything which mind can exchange with mind that is not knowledge, in the usual sense, but rather some state of feeling. Then we see very quickly that, while knowledge is of many kinds, it is divisible as a whole into two great, widely different species, the line between which is an interesting one to notice. One of those species we may call the *knowledge of what has been*, and the other we will describe as the *knowledge of what is*. The first is knowledge of the past; the second is knowledge of the present. The first is History ; the second is (using the word in a large sense) Science. We are not straining the term Science if we make it cover everything, in philosophy, politics, economics, arts, that is not historical ; and we shall not be straining the term Poetry if we use that to represent everything which we have left out of the category of positive knowledge, being everything that belongs to imagination and emotion.

In History, Science, Poetry, then, we name the most obvious assorting of the matter known as Literature, of which books are the necessary carriers. But there is another classification of it, not often considered, which is a more important one, in my view, and which exhibits the function of books much more impressively. Draw one broad line through everything that mind can receive from mind, — everything, — memory, thought, imagination, suggestion, — and put on one side of it all that has come from the

past, against everything, on the other
side, that comes from the present, and
then meditate a little on what it signifies!
In our first classification we considered
the past only with reference to history,
or knowledge *of* the past. Now, I wish
to put with that all of our knowledge, of
every kind, that has come to us *out of* the
past; and when you have reflected a
moment you will see that that means almost everything that we know. For all
the knowledge now in the possession of
mankind has been a slow accumulation,
going on through not less than seventy
centuries. Each succeeding generation
has learned just a little that was new, to
add to what it received from the generations before, and has passed the inherit-
ance on with a trivial increase. We are
apt to look rather scornfully at any science which is dated before 1900. But
where would our brand-new discoveries
have been without the older ones which
led up to them by painful steps? In nine

cases out of ten it was an eye of genius that caught the early glimpses of things which dull eyes can see plainly enough now.

Most of the science, then, which we value so in these days, has come to us, in the train of all history, out of the past; and poetry, too, has come with it, and music, and the great laws of righteousness, without which we could be little better than the beasts. How vast an estate it is that we come into as the intellectual heirs of all the watchers and searchers and thinkers and singers of the generations that are dead! What a heritage of stored wealth! What perishing poverty of mind we should be left in without it!

Now, books are the carriers of all this accumulating heritage from generation to generation; and that, I am sure you will agree with me, is their most impressive function. It will bear thinking of a little further.

You and I, who live at this moment,

stand islanded, so to speak, on a narrow strand between two great time-oceans, — the ocean of Time Past and the ocean of Time to Come. When we turn to one, looking future-ward, we see nothing — not even a ripple on the face of the silent, mysterious deep, which is veiled by an impenetrable mist. We turn backward to the other sea, looking out across the measureless expanse of Time Past, and, lo! it is covered with ships. We see them rise from beyond the far horizon in fleets which swarm upon the scene, and they come sailing to us in numbers that are greater than we can count. They are freighted with the gifts of the dead, to us who are the children of the dead. They bring us the story of the forgotten life of mankind, its experience, its learning, its wisdom, its warnings, its counsels, its consolations, its songs, its discoveries of beauty and joy. What if there had been no ships to bring us these? Think of it! What if the great ocean of Time Past rolled as blankly and blackly behind us as the ocean of Time to Come rolls before us? What if there were no letters and no books? For the ships in this picture are those carriers of the commodities of mind which we call Letters and Books.

Think what your state would be in a situation like that! Think what it would be to know nothing, for example, of the way in which American Independence was won, and the federal republic of the United States constructed; nothing of Bunker Hill; nothing of George Washington, — except the little, half true and half mistaken, that your fathers could remember, of what their fathers had repeated, of what *their* fathers had told to them! Think what it would be to have nothing but shadowy traditions of the voyage of Columbus, of the coming of the Mayflower pilgrims, and of all the planting of life in the New World from Old World stocks, — like Greek legends of the Argonauts and of the Heraclidæ!

Think what it would be to know no more
of the origins of the English people, their
rise and their growth in greatness, than
the Romans knew of their Latin beginnings ; and to know no more of Rome
herself than we might guess from the
ruins she has left! Think what it would
be to have the whole story of Athens and
Greece dropped out of our knowledge,
and to be unaware that Marathon was
ever fought, or that one like Socrates had
ever lived! Think what it would be to
have no line from Homer, no thought
from Plato, no message from Isaiah, no
Sermon on the Mount, nor any parable
from the lips of Jesus!

Can you imagine a world intellectually
famine-smitten like that — a bookless
world — and not shrink with horror from
the thought of being condemned to it?

Yet, — and here is the grim fact which
I am most anxious to impress on your
thought, — the men and the women who
take nothing from letters and books are

choosing to live as though mankind did actually wallow in the awful darkness of that state from which writing and books have rescued us. For them, it is as if no ship had ever come from the far shores of old Time where their ancestry dwelt; and the interest of existence to them is huddled in the petty space of their own few years, between walls of mist which thicken as impenetrably behind them as before. How can life be worth living on such terms as that? How can men or women be content with so little, when they might have so much?

I have dwelt long enough on the generalized view of books, their function and their value. It is time that I turned to more definite considerations.

You will expect me, no doubt, to say something of the relative value of books, to indicate some principles in choosing them, and to mark, perhaps, some lines for reading. There must always be a difficulty in that undertaking for any person who would give advice to others concerning books, though his knowledge of them surpassed mine a hundredfold. For the same book has never the same value for all minds, and scarcely two readers can follow the same course in their reading with the same good. There is a personal bent of mind which ought to have its way in this matter, so far as a deliberate judgment in the mind itself will allow. So far, that is, as one can willingly do it who desires the fullest culture that his mind is capable of receiving, he should humor its inclinations. Against an eager delight in poetry, for example, he should not force himself, I am sure, to an obstinate reading of science ; nor vice versa. But the lover of poetry who neglects science entirely, and the devotee of science who scorns acquaintance with poetry, are equally guilty of a foolish mutilation of themselves. The man of science needs, even for a large apprehension of scientific truth, and still more for a large and healthy development of his own being, that best exercise of imagination which true poetry alone can give. The man of poetic nature, on the other hand, needs the discipline of judgment and reason for which exact learning of some kind is indispensable.

So inclination is a guide to follow, in reading as in other pursuits, with extremest caution; and there is one favorite direction in which we can never trust it safely. That is down the smooth way of indolent amusement, where the gardens of weedy romance are, and the fields in which idle gossip is gathered by farmers of news. Of the value of romance in true literature, and of the intellectual worth of that knowledge of passing events which is news in the real sense, I may possibly say something before I am done. I touch them now only to remark, that the inclination which draws many people so easily into a dissipated reading of trashy novels and puerile news-gossip is something very different from the inclination of mind which carries some to science, some to history, some to poetry. In the latter there is a turn of intellect, a push of special faculties, a leaning of taste, which demand respect, as I have said. The former is nothing more than one kind of the infirmity which produces laziness in all its modes. The state of a novel-steeped mind is just that of a lounging, lolling, slouching body, awake and alive enough for some superficial pleasant tickling of sense-consciousness, but with all energy drained out of it and all the joy of strength in action unknown. It is a loaferish mind that can loll by the hour over trash and trivialities in a novel or a newspaper.

To come back to the question of choice among good books: there is a certain high region in all departments of literature which every reader who cares to make the most of himself and

the best of life ought to penetrate and
become in some measure acquainted
with, whatever his personal leanings may
be. It is the region of the *great* books —
the greatest, that is, of the greater kinds.
For the realm of literature is a vast universe of solar systems — of suns and sat-
ellites; and, while no man can hope
to explore it all, he may seek and find
the central sources of light in it and take
an illumination from them which no reflected rays can give. In poetry (which
I must speak of again), I doubt if many
people can read very much of minor
verse — the verse of merely ingenious
fancies and melodious lines — with intellectual benefit, whatever pleasure it may
afford them. But the *great* poems, which
fuse thought and imagination into one
glorified utterance, will carry an enrichment beyond measuring into any mind
that has capacity to receive them. I believe that those fortunate young people
who are wise enough, or wisely enough

directed, to engrave half of Shakespeare
upon their memories, lastingly, in their
youth, with something of Milton, something of Goethe, something of Wordsworth, something of Keats, something of
Tennyson, something of Browning, something of Dante, something of Homer and
the Greek dramatists, with much of Hebrew poetry from the Bible, have made
a noble beginning of the fullest and
finest culture that is possible. To mem-
orize great poems in early life is to lay
a store in the mind for which its happy
possessor can never be too thankful in
after years. I speak from experience,
not of the possession of such a store,
but of the want of it. I have felt the want
greatly since I came to years when memory will not take deposits graciously,
nor keep them with faithfulness, and I
warn you that if these riches are to be
yours at all you must gather them in
your youth.

A great poem is like a mountain top,

which invites one toward the heavens,
into a new atmosphere, and a new vision
of the world, and a new sense of being.
There are no other equal heights in literature except those which have been attained by a few teachers of the divinest
truth, who have borne messages of righteousness to mankind. Even as literature,
to be read for nothing more than their
quality and their influence as such, what
can compare with the parables and dis-
courses of Jesus, as reported in the
Gospels? I know of nothing else that
comes nearer to them than a few of the
dialogues of Plato, which exhibit the character and represent the higher teachings
of Socrates. The three dialogues called
the "Apology," the "Crito," and the
"Phædo," which tell the sublime story of
the trial and death of Socrates, are writings that I would put next to the books
of the Evangelists in the library of every
young reader. They were published
separately a few years ago, in a small,

attractive volume, under the title of "The
Trial and Death of Socrates," and they
are also to be found in the second volume of the fine translation of Plato made
by Professor Jowett. Another selection of
half a dozen of the best of the Socratic
dialogues can be had in a charming little
book entitled "Talks with Athenian
Youths." By the side of these, I would
put the "Thoughts" of the Emperor
Marcus Aurelius and the "Enchiridion"
of Epictetus; and not far from them I
would place the "Essays" of Lord Bacon
and of our own wise Emerson.

These are books, not of mere Knowledge, but of Wisdom, which is far above
Knowledge. Knowledge is brought *into*
the mind; Wisdom is from its own
springs. Knowledge is the fruit of learning; Wisdom is the fruit of meditation.
Knowledge is related to the facts of life,
and to man in his dependence on them;
Wisdom is concerned with life itself, and
with man in his own being. Knowledge

equips us for our duties and tasks ; Wisdom lights them up for us. The great meditative books, such as these I have named, are books that have lifted, exalted, illuminated millions of minds, and their power will never be spent. A book of science grows stale with age, and is superseded by another. The book of wisdom can never grow old. But in this age of science it is apt to be neglected, and therefore I speak with some pleading for it. Do not pass it by in your reading.

In what I say to you, I am thinking of books as we use them in *reading*, not in *study*. Study has some special cultivation of mind or particular acquisition in view ; reading is a more general, discursive, and lighter pursuit of the good that is in books. Now, it is looking at them in that way, broadly, that I will make a few suggestions about books which belong in what I have classed as the literature of knowledge. I would award the highest place in that class to history, because it gives more exercise than any other, not alone to every faculty of our intelligence, — to our reason, our judgment, our memory, and our imagination, — but to every moral sensibility we possess. But if history is to be read with that effect, it must not be read as a mere collection of stories of war and battle, revolution and adventure. It must not be traversed as one strolls through a picture gallery, looking at one thing in a frame here, and another thing in a frame there, — an episode depicted by this historian, an epoch by that one, the career of a nation by a third, — each distinct from every other, in its own framing, and considered in itself. To read history in that way is to lose all its meaning and teaching. On the contrary, we must keep always in our minds a view of history as one great whole, and the chief interest we find in it should be that of discovering the connection and relation of each part to other parts. Of course we have to pick up our knowledge of it in pieces and sections; but only so fast as we can put them together, and acquire a wide, comprehensive survey of events and movements, in many countries, will historical knowledge become real knowledge to us, and its interest and value be disclosed to our minds. We see then what a seamless web it is, woven, as Goethe describes it, in " the roaring loom of time," of unbroken threads which stretch from the beginning of the life of men on the earth, and which will spin onward to the end. We read then the history of our own country as a part of the history of the English people, and the history of the English people as a part of the history of the Germanic race, and Germanic history in its close sequence to Roman history, and Roman history as the outcome of conditions which trace back to Greece and the ancient East. We read the thrilling narrative of our great civil war, not as a tragical story which begins at Sumter and ends at Appomattox, but as the tremendous catastrophe of a long, inflexible series of effects and causes which runs back from the New World into the Old, and through centuries of time, slowly engendering the conflict which exploded at last in the rebellion of a slave-holding self-interest against the hard-won supremacy of a national conscience.

Concerning history, then, I come back again, with special emphasis, to the counsel I gave generally before : read the *great* books, which spread it out for you in large views. Whatever you may seek in the way of minute details and close studies, here and there, for this and that period and country, get a general groundwork for them in your mind from the comprehensive surveys of the great historians. Above all, read Gibbon. If you would comprehend modern history, you *must* read his " Decline and Fall of the Roman Empire." It is the one fundamental work. Though it is old, nothing supersedes it. It is an unequaled, unapproached panorama of more than a thousand years of time, crowded with the most pregnant events, on the central stage of human history. Whatever else you read or do not read, you cannot afford to neglect Gibbon.

Of the ages before Gibbon's period, in Roman, Greek, and Oriental history, there is nothing which offers a really large, comprehensive survey. But Maspero, Sayce, McCurdy, Thirlwall, Grote, Curtius, Mahaffy, Mommsen, Merivale, are of the best. For a brief, clear account of the Roman Republic, sketching its inner rather than its surface history, I know of nothing else so good as Horton's "History of the Roman People."

Generally, as regards ancient history, there is a warning which I find to be needed. Within quite recent years, the discoveries that have been made, by digging into buried ruins of old cities, bringing to light and comparing great numbers of records from the remotest times, preserved by their inscription on earthen tablets and on stone, have so added to and so corrected our knowledge of ancient history that the narratives of the older historians have become of little worth. It is an utter waste of time, for example, to read the venerable Rollin, new editions of whose history are still being published and sold. You might as well go to Ptolemy for astronomy, or to Aristotle for physical science. It is a worse waste of time to read Abbott histories, and their kind. Beware of them.

Mediæval history, too, and many periods more modern, have received new light which discredits more or less the historians who were trusted a generation or two ago. Hallam is found to be wrong in important parts of his view of the institutions of feudalism. Hume is seen to give untrue representations of English political history at some of its chief turning points. Macaulay has done frequent injustice in his powerful arraignment of great actors on the British stage. The study and the writing of history have become more painstaking, more accurate, more dispassionate, less partisan and less eloquent, but more just. We get the surest and broadest views of it in Freeman, Stubbs, Maitland, Green, Gairdner, Gardiner, Ranke, May, Lecky, and Seeley for English history, with Bagehot to describe the present working of the English Constitution.

In continental history, mediæval and modern, I will mention just a few among many of the books which I think can be recommended safely : Church's " Beginnings of the Middle Ages," Emerton's " Mediæval Europe," Bryce's " Holy Roman Empire," some of Freeman's " Historical Essays," Milman's "History of Latin Christianity," Symonds's " Renaissance in Italy," Trollope's " Commonwealth of Florence," Ranke's and

Creighton's histories of the Papacy in the sixteenth and seventeenth centuries, Häusser's "Period of the Reformation," Baird's Huguenot histories, Motley's "Rise of the Dutch Republic" and "United Netherlands," Gindely or Gardiner's "Thirty Years War," Perkins's "France under Mazarin," "France under the Regency," and "France under Louis XV.," Rocquain's "Revolutionary Spirit Preceding the Revolution," Prof. Henry Morse Stephen's "French Revolution," Fournier's "Napoleon," Thayer's "Dawn of Italian Independence," Andrews's "Historical Development of Modern Europe," and the series by different writers, entitled "Periods of European History," edited by Arthur Hassell. Moreover, the little books in the series called "Epochs of English History" and "Epochs of Modern History" are almost all of them excellent.

Into American history it is best, for several reasons, that we, of this country, should go more thoroughly than into that of other countries. One who tries to get his knowledge of it from a single book or two will remain very ignorant. The best of the general narratives which attempt to cover the whole, from Columbus, or even from Captain John Smith, to President McKinley, are only sketches that need to be filled. For many parts of that filling, the series of volumes now in course of publication under the general editorship of Professor Hart, of Harvard University, in which successive periods and movements are treated by different writers, can be recommended safely. "The American Nation: A History," is the title of the series. But take from John Fiske, I would say, his colonial histories, — especially " Old Virginia and her Neighbours " and " The Dutch and Quaker Colonies," — and his story of " The American Revolution," together with that of " The Critical Period " which followed it, down to the adoption of the Fed-

eral Constitution. For your own delight
you should linger long enough in colonial times to read all that Parkman has
written of the French in America and of
their great effort to possess the continent.
Irving, in his " Life of Washington," and
McMaster, in his " History of the People
of the United States," will give you a good
knowledge of the first years of the republic ; but you will never understand Jeffer-
son and Madison, and the rise of the great
old political parties, and the War of 1812
with England, if you do not read the history written by Henry Adams, which cov-
ers the time between John Adams and
Monroe. For the next third of a century,
I would trust to Holst's " Constitutional
and Political History," and Professor
Burgess's history of " The Middle Period," as it is named in the " American
History Series." These works are made
needlessly hard reading by their style,
but they are full of good instruction.
With them I would place half a dozen

of the biographies in the series of the "American Statesmen," for side lights thrown upon the politics of the time. Then take Rhodes's "History of the United States from the Compromise of 1850," which carries you through and beyond the civil war. For that great struggle I consider Nicolay and Hay's "Abraham Lincoln" to be, on the whole, the best history that has been written yet. It is a huge work, in many volumes, but no one who reads it will waste time or easily tire. Along with it should be read the collected writings of Abraham Lincoln, which are the most lasting literature, excepting, perhaps, Emerson's "Essays," that America has produced. As a whole series of state papers, I believe that the speeches, letters, messages, and proclamations of President Lincoln are the most extraordinary, in wisdom, in spirit, and in composition, that ever came, in any country or any age, from the tongue and pen of one man. You will find it an education, both in literature and in politics, to read them again and again. Read, too, the simply and nobly written " Personal Memoirs," of General Grant, with those of Sherman, Sheridan, and Joe Johnston, Long's " Life of Lee," Blaine's " Twenty Years in Congress," and your knowledge of rebellion history will be quite complete. Then cap your reading in this region of history and politics with Bryce's " American Commonwealth," and I would have no great desire to urge more.

Biography is in one sense a part of history ; but that which interests us in it most, and from which we take the most good, if we take any, is more than historical. The story of a life which offers nothing but its incidents, informs us of nothing but its achievements, was never worth the telling. Fill it with romance, or glorify it with great triumphs, and still there is small worth in it. If he who lived the life is not in himself more interesting and more significant to us than all the circumstance of his life, then the circumstance is vainly set forth. What biography at its best can give us, as the finest form of history, and as more than history, is the personal revelation, the in-seen portraiture of here and there a human soul which is not common in its quality. The exemplars that it sets most abundantly before us, of a vulgar kind of practical success in the world, — the success of a mere self-seeking talent and industry applied to private business or to public affairs, — are well enough in their way, and may make some small impressions of good effect on some minds; but we take no inspiration from them — they give us no ideals. What we ought to seek everywhere in books is escape from the commonplace — the commonplace in thought and the commonplace in character with which our daily life surrounds us. Our chief dependence is on books to bring us into intercourse with the picked, choice examples of human kind;

to show us what they *are* or what they have *been*, as well as what they have thought, — what they have done, as well as what they have said, — with what motives, from what impulses, with what powers, to what ends, in what spirit, the work of their lives has been done. When biography does that for us it is one of the most precious forms of literature. But when it only crams our library shelves with " process-print " pictures, so to speak, of commonplace characters in commonplace settings of life, we waste time in reading it. I know people who relish biography as they would relish gossip in talk, delighting in disclosures from other men's and other women's lives, no matter how trivial, and all the more, perhaps, when some spicing of scandal is in them. So far as it invites reading in that spirit there is nothing to commend it. But I have never known one person who enjoyed what may be called the fine flavors of character in biography who had not fine tastes in all literature.

The composition of biography would seem to be one of the most difficult of literary arts, since masterpieces in it are so few. The delightful and noble subjects that have been offered it in every age of the world are abounding in number, but how many have been worthily treated? One can almost count on his fingers the biographical works that hold a classic place in common esteem. Generally, of the best and greatest and most beautiful lives that have been lived there is no story which communicates the grandeur or the charm as we ought to be made to feel it.

The most famous of biographies, that of Doctor Samuel Johnson by his admiring friend Boswell, has a strong and striking personality for its subject; but who can read it without wishing that some figure more impressive in human history stood where a strange fortune has put the sturdy old Tory, in the wonderful light that reveals him so immortally? Among literary men, Sir Walter Scott has come nearer, perhaps, than any other to Doctor Johnson's good fortune, in the life of him written by Lockhart, his son-in-law. Trevelyan's " Life and Letters of Macaulay," and the " Memoirs of Charles Kingsley" by his wife, are probably the best of later examples in literary biography. But in a certain view all the more eminent " Men of Letters," English and American, may be called biographically fortunate since the publication in England and America of the two series of small biographies so named. It is true that these are rather to be looked upon as critical studies and sketches than as biographies in the adequate sense; but most of them are remarkably good in their way, and for these busy days of many books they may suffice. The same is true of the " Twelve English States-men" series in political biography, as

well as of the series of " American States-
men," alluded to before.

Using the term "study" in the sense
in which artists use it, when, for example,
they distinguish between a portrait and
a "study of a head," I should apply it
to a large class of biographical sketches
which are as true to literary art as the
most finished biography could be, and
only lack its completeness in detail. The
prototype of all such writings is found in
".Plutarch's Lives," which are studies —
comparative studies — of the great characters of antiquity, and models to this day
of their kind. As we have them in Dry-
den's translation revised by Clough, or
in the old translation by North which
Shakespeare used, there is no better reading for old or for young.

Scientific biography is at its best, I
should say, in the "Life and Letters
of Charles Darwin," by his son. In the
" Life and Letters " of Huxley, the letters
are delightful, and the story of the life

is most interesting, despite a lack of skill in the telling. The "Life of Thomas Edward," the humble Scotch naturalist, by Doctor Samuel Smiles, is hardly to be surpassed as a book of edification and delight, especially for the young. Smiles's "Life of Robert Dick" is nearly but not quite as good; and the "Autobiography of James Nasmyth," man of science and great engineer, edited by the same skillful hand, is one of the books which I never lose an opportunity to press upon boys, for the sake of the wonderful example it sets before them, of a thoughtful plan of life perseveringly carried out, from beginning to end. Other works of Smiles in industrial biography — lives of Watts, the Stephensons, and many more — are all exceptionally interesting and wholesome to read.

Franklin's autobiography, in the same line of interest and influence, is one of the books which the world would be greatly poorer without. Grimm's "Life of Michael Angelo " takes a kindred lesson of life and lifts it to a setting more heroic. Goethe's autobiography and his " Conversations with Eckermann " are of the books that stamp themselves ineffaceably on a receptive mind, and that ought to be read before the enthusiasms of youth are outworn.

But I am particularizing books much more than it was my intention to do. I had planned a hasty excursion along the watersheds of literature, so to speak, just to notice some features of the geography of the world of books, and point here and there to a monument that seemed important in my view. To assume to be really a guide for any other reading than my own is more than I am willing to undertake.

II

THE TEST OF QUALITY IN BOOKS

one hand, the springs of all art, — music, poetry, romance, drama, sculpture, painting, — brimmed with delights of the imagination and the joy of the beauty of the world ; on the other hand, the muddy wells into which so many people choose perversely to dip. From these two fountains of pleasure-giving art, one polluted and the other pure, the differing streams are ever flowing. Which of them has floated to us an offered book of entertainment is what we must know, if we can.

Whether the book is alive with genius or dead with the lack of it, — whether it is brilliant or commonplace, — whether clumsiness or skill is in the construction of it, — are not the first questions to be asked. The prior question, as I conceive, is this : *Does the book leave any kind of wholesome and fine feeling in the mind of one who reads it ?* That is not a question concerning the mere morality of the book, in the conventional meaning of the term. It touches the whole quality of the work as one of true literature. "Does it leave any kind of wholesome and fine feeling in the mind of one who reads it?" There is no mistaking a feeling of that nature, though it may never seem twice the same in our experience of it. Sometimes it may be to us as though we had eaten of good food; at other times like the tasting of wine; at others, again, like a draught of water from a cool spring. Some books that we read will make us feel that we are lifted as on wings; some will make music within us; some will give us visions; some will just fill us with a happy content. In such feelings there is a refining potency that seems to be equaled in nothing else. The simplest art is as sure to produce them as the highest. We take them from Burns's lines "To a Field-Mouse," from Wordsworth's "Poor Susan," from the story of Ruth, from the story of "The Vicar of Wakefield," from the story of "Picciola," from the story of "Daddy Darwin's Dovecot,"

as certainly as from " Hamlet " or from
" Henry Esmond." The true pleasure,
the fine pleasure, the civilizing pleasure
to be drawn from any form of art is one
which leaves a distinctly wholesome feeling of some such nature as these that I
have tried to describe ; and the poem, the
romance, the play, the music, or the picture, which has nothing of the sort to
give us, but only a moment of sensation
and then blankness, does us no kind of
good, however innocent of positive evil
it may be.

If the wholesome feeling which all true
art produces, in literature or elsewhere, is
unmistakable, so, too, are those feelings
of the other nature which works of an op-
posite character give rise to. Our minds
are as sensitive to a moral force of gravi-
tation as our bodies are sensitive to the
physical force, and we are as conscious
of the downward pull upon us of a vulgar
tale or a vicious play as we are conscious
of the buoyant lift of one that is nobly

written. We have likewise a mental touch, to which the texture of coarse literature is a fact as distinct as the grit in a muddy road that we grind with our heels. And so I will say again that the conclusive test for a book which offers pleasure rather than knowledge is in the question, " Does it leave any kind of wholesome and fine feeling in the mind of one who reads it ? "

All this which I am saying is opposed to a doctrine preached in our day, by a school of pretenders in art, whose chatter has made too much impression on careless minds. It appeared first, I believe, among the painters, in France, and French literature took infection from it; then England became somewhat diseased, and America is not without peril. It is the false doctrine which phrases itself in the meaningless motto — " Art for Art's sake ! " " Pursue Art for Art's sake," — " Enjoy Art for Art's sake," cry these æsthetic prophets, who have no compre-

hension of what Art **is**. As well talk of
sailing a ship for the ship's sake, — of
wheeling a cart for the cart's sake, — of
articulating words for the words' sake.
Art is a vessel, a vehicle, for the carriage
and communication of something from
one mind to another mind, — from one
soul to another soul. Without a content,
it has no more reason for its being than
a meaningless word could have in human
speech. Considered in itself and for its
own sake, it has no existence ; it is an
imposture — a mere simulation of Art ;
for that which would be Art, if filled duly
with meanings and laden with a message, is then but an artisan's handicraft.

The truth is, there are cunning deceits
in this pretension to " Art for Art's sake."
Those who lead the cry for it do not
mean what their words seem to imply.
They do not mean the emptiness that one
might suppose. What they do mean, as
a rule, is to put something ignoble in the
place of what should be noble ; some-

thing vulgar or something vile in the place of what should be wholly pure and wholly fine. What they really strive to do is to degrade the content of Art, and to persuade the world that it can be made the vehicle of mean ideals without ceasing to be Art in the noble sense. The workers to that end in literature are very busy, and I suggest this as an important rule in the choosing of books : Beware of the literature of the school which preaches "Art for Art's sake."

III

HINTS AS TO READING

HINTS AS TO READING[1]

I MAY take for granted, in what I say this evening, that no one who hears me is indifferent to what Mr. Maurice has called "the friendship of books," nor requires to be persuaded that the reading of good books is an occupation of time so delightful and so profitable that hardly any other can be preferred to it. I may take that for granted, because it is fair to assume that no one who feels indifferent or repugnant to books would come to hear them talked about. And I am glad that it is so ; because I should have no faith to encourage me in speaking to people of that mind. I should not hope to make books appear attractive to any man or any woman who has grown to maturity without feeling the charm of them. I

[1] From a lecture.

would do so most gladly if I could; for
not many misfortunes appeal to me more.
To know nothing of the friendship that
never fails, the companionship that never
tires, the entertainment that is never far
to seek nor costly to command, the
blessed resource that can save every precious hour of life from the dreadful wickedness of "the killing of Time," — what
poverty is greater than that!

Assuming that the worth and the
charm of books are undisputed in this
company, there is nothing in question
here except the discriminations to be exercised among them. I am to offer you
such suggestions as I can concerning the
reading of books and the choice of books
for reading. For *reading*, be it remembered, not for *study*. The distinction between readers and students is one that I
wish to keep in mind. The student, as
we think of him, stands for the scholar,
to whom books are the business of life,
first and before all things, — fundamen-

tal, — implemental, — professional. The reader, on the other hand, has something else for vocation and chief employment, and his book is a happy incident, which night brings to him, perhaps, with his slippers, his easy-chair, and his lamp. What he asks from it is not scholarship, but a well-rounded knowledge, — a wholesome culture, — a quickened imagination, — a mind nourished and refreshed. We may all be readers, even to a large, broad measure of the term ; but not many can be students and scholars, in the completer sense. Yet some fraction of true scholarship ought to be perfected in every one.

And this, in fact, is the first suggestion I am moved to make, — namely, that, while it is both necessary and better for the majority of people that they should be readers of books in a general way, rather than students and specialists of learning, it is better still that the reading of each one should range with wide free-

dom round some centre of actual study,
some chapter of history, some question,
some language, some work or some personality in literature, — it scarcely matters what, so long as a little definite
province of knowledge is really occupied
and possessed, while larger territories
around it are only reconnoitred and over-
run. I say it is better for the majority of
people that they should be readers in a
general way, rather than students, because they have not the leisure nor the
freedom of mind for large subjects of
study, and it is ill for the mind to focus
it on small themes too exclusively.
Among teachers and original investi-
gators the specialization of learning becomes every day more necessary, as the
bulk of science increases ; but every spe-
cialist puts his soul in peril, so to speak,
by the risk of narrowed faculties and an
intellectual myopia to which he is ex-
posed. So I would not, for my own part,
give a word of encouragement to that

growing class of people who may be
called the class of *amateur specialists;* because their exclusive devotion to special
subjects seems too little and too much;—
too little, that is, for any service to human
knowledge, and too much for the best
development of themselves. I feel no
doubt, in the least, that breadth of culture
is more important, on the whole, than its
depth, to the generality of mankind ; that
their character and capability as mem-
bers of society are affected more by the
area of their knowledge and by the diver-
sity of their acquaintance with good literature, than by the minuteness of either.

At the same time, I would urge, as I
say, the specializing of some object in the
intellectual pursuits of every man and
woman; not to the exclusion of other
subjects and objects, but to their subor-
dination. Let there be one thing for each
of us that we try to know somewhere
nearly to the bottom, with certainty, precision, exactness ; not so much for the

value of the knowledge itself, as for the value of the discipline of thoroughness. If it is something in the line of our daily occupations, — something bearing upon our particular work in the world, mechanical, commercial, professional, whatever it maybe, — so much the better. Then, around that one centre of positive study, turning on it as on a pivot, let there be circle after circle drawn of wide discursive reading.

If this seems to be a doctrine that is too indulgent of easy habits in reading, and too favorable to superficiality, I will hasten to introduce a second suggestion which cannot be so suspected. It shall be more than a suggestion, for I would make it a very serious admonition and injunction to all who will give attention to me on this subject : Be temperate in Newspapers ! For there is an intemperance in the newspaper-reading of the day which looks nearly as threatening to me as the intemperance that is fed from

the brewery and the still. To a certain
extent, — and I would not be narrow in
measuring it, — good newspapers are to
be rated with good books, and even before them in one view, because no other
reading is so indispensable to the education that accords with the conditions
of life at the present day. I value as
highly as one reasonably can the wonderful news-knowledge of our time. It is
sweeping so much pettiness, so much
small provincialism, out of the feeling and
thinking of men, making them cosmo-
politan, coöperative, tolerant! With the
whole world gathered into one neighbor-
hood, so to speak, and the daily story of
its doings and happenings made the talk
of the breakfast-table, morning by morning, and the chat of the club and the sit-
ting-room evening by evening; with the
calamities of Asia, the catastrophes of
the South Sea, the tragedies of Muscovy,
the agitations of Paris, the politics of
London, the sensations of New York,

poured hourly into our consciousness, along with the passing events of our own lives and of the little circles in which we revolve, — how can we fail to outgrow in our sympathies and ideas the provincial boundaries that were hard and fast for earlier men? It is a mighty factor in modern education, this flying world-news that takes wings from the daily press and is gathered from the uttermost parts of the earth.

But the staple of it, after all, is *gossip*; — world-gossip, to be sure, — history-gossip in great part, — but *gossip*, nevertheless; and overmuch of it is thin nourishment for any robust and capable mind. Unwholesome, too, as well as thin. There is a kind of moral narcotism common to every species of gossip, high or low, which takes possession, like an opium-habit, of the minds that are much given to it, and works degeneracy in them. Who can mistake the morbid effects in that direction which appear in the news-

paper-reading world, and which seem
to be magnified from day to day? The
craving for coarser flavors in the news-
reports; for more pungency of sensation;
more photography of vice; more dram-
atization of crime; more puerile personality; more spying and eaves-dropping;
more invasion and desecration of the pri-
vacies and sacred things of life; — that
insatiable craving, which popular journalism panders to, seems to have an incessant growth from what it feeds on,
and one shudders in imagining the pitch
of enterprise and audacity to which reporters may yet be pushed by it. The
fault is no more than half on the side of
the newspapers; it belongs as much, or
more, to the readers for whose taste the
popular newspapers are made up; and I
am convinced that, if we track home this
disease of taste which is gluttonous of the
garbage of news, we shall find it mostly
among people whose sole literature is
from the daily and hebdomadal press;

who read newspapers and nothing else. They constitute a great class, and I fear it is a growing class, — in this country more, perhaps, than in any other. We are called "a reading people;" but a newspaper-reading people may be the truer description; and neither we nor our newspapers, as I have tried to indicate, are improved by the excess of interest in them.

Let us read the news of the day, by all means. Let us never fail to keep abreast of it, in fair acquaintance with the current movements of event and opinion, maintaining and cultivating a healthy interest in the affairs of the world, great and small, and in the doing, feeling, and thinking of our living fellow men. But let us be temperate in it; let us not saturate ourselves with the sensations of the passing day. Let us reserve some room in our minds for a knowledge of the past, its ideas and its history, and of present things that are not caught by the reporter's pencil or the editor's pen.

I have placed intemperance in newspaper-reading even before intemperance
in novel-reading, because I look upon it
as the more serious of the two; but the
latter is a very grave evil, contributing
to a mental and moral debility which we
must not treat lightly. Understand that
I speak only of intemperance in novel-
reading, or of intemperance and ill-selec-
tion together; for I am not of those who
despise the novel, or condemn it in a
sweeping way. In my view it has its
place among the higher forms of literature, — of literature as art, — and so far
as it is made fitting to that high place,
by the genius which has a right to create
it, the novel is a gift to be welcomed and
enjoyed. In the reading of a young person I would not withhold a fair — even a
liberal — proportion of wholesome and
finely woven romance. We must not be
of the school of the Gradgrinds. Some
nutriment is demanded for our souls besides the nutriment of facts. The intel-

lectual life is not all remembering, or all reckoning and reasoning. It includes feeling and imagination, and we need to cultivate that side of our nature no less than the other, for a rounded, sane development of ourselves. We need to cultivate it, moreover, by other means and from other sources than books. Nature, to those who read her, is more eloquent than any poem; and no love-tale is so interesting as the every-day life that we have under our eyes. Yet the poetry and romance in books have a singular importance in this region of culture, because, if we choose them well, they can bring to us the reinforcement of imaginations that are greater than our own, and touch us through sensibilities and sympathies that are finer than we possess. If they do not that, they can do us no good, and we may better leave them unread.

What I say of romance need only be writ larger for poetry, and it is equally true. A true poem — the simplest true poem — will bring something to us that is a revelation; some glimpse that we never had before of a meaning in things that lights them up to us ; or some thrill of an emotion which attunes us in newly felt relations with God, or Nature, or Man. There is no true poetry which does not that; and the idle rhyme that has only the lilt in it of a few dancing words, or the sparkle of a few trifling fancies, will defraud us of the time spent in reading it. Read pure, true poetry, as you would open your window on a morning in June; as you would walk in a garden when the flowers are spread, or into the fields when the corn is ripe; as you would go up to the mountains, or out on the shore of the sea. Go to it for the light and the gladness and the bloom of beauty and the larger horizons and the sweeter atmosphere you can find in it, for the rest and refreshment and revivifying of your souls.

What is not read for the kinds of practical knowledge that we call *information* is to be read for some such good to one's soul, if there is anything of worth in its print. Facts for our store of practical knowledge ; teachings and exercises for our understanding and reason ; illumination and inspiration for the spiritualities that are in us ; wholesome stimulants for our lighter sensibilities, of fancy and of humor and the like, — these are the differing kinds of good for which we can go to books, and one or the other of which we should require them to supply. We know when they answer the demand ; generally we know when they fail. Teachings, illuminations, inspirations, are unmistakable experiences of mind ; but the wholesome gratifications of fancy and humor are not always so distinguishable from the unwholesome, and it is there that the flood of modern fiction brings difficulty into the question of books. It is a difficulty which each reader must prepare to overcome, in the main, for himself. The discriminating sense — the feeling for what is good and for what is not good in the vast output of novel-writing at the present day — can be trained by exercising it on the undisputed classics of fiction that we inherit from the past. One who reads Cervantes, Defoe, Scott, Dickens, Thackeray, George Eliot, Charles Kingsley, Erckmann-Chatrian, and others of the " old masters " of romance, till they have grooved habits of taste in his mind, is not likely to be cheated by any prentice-work, tricked out in later styles.

And the more substantial literature, — the concrete literature of fact, — what shall I say of that? I am not here to urge people into this course of reading or that, dictated, as the counsel would naturally be, by my own inclinations of taste. There can be no kind or course of reading that is best for all. The bent of each mind is to be yielded to; not wholly, but so far as will determine the main direction pursued : as to whether it shall be in history, or travel, or natural science, or social science, or philosophy, or art. Embarrassed as we are by the multitude and variety of things that claim attention in the world, we *may*, any of us, neglect philosophy, or the arts, or half the sciences ; but we *must* read something of history, if we are to understand at all the stage on which we are acting, — the plot of the drama of life in which we are playing parts, — the world and the humanity to which we belong. And there are some suggestions on that point that I am glad to have an opportunity to make.

First, I would say, give a little attention — more than is given commonly — to the background of history. It is one of the discoveries of recent times that there is such a thing as a background to history. Our ancestors knew of nothing behind the written annals of mankind, except the mist-cloud of fables from which they start. For us, however, there is accumulated already a wonderful body of prehistoric knowledge, more or less conjecturable and debatable, to be sure, but exceedingly significant, nevertheless, throwing flashes of light into the dim dawns of civilization and society. It is made up of a multitude of hints and fragments of fact, picked here and there out of the roots of old languages and the kitchen - heaps, cave - relics, and burial-mounds of primitive savage men, which are found to have surprising meanings when they are put together and compared and construed. To learn what we are able to learn from them, concerning the early divisions, relations, and movements of the tribes and races of mankind, before any kind of written record was made, or any name or personal figure appears, to produce for us the first dim picture of living history, is to acquire a most important ground of understanding for the recorded history that starts out from it later on.

Even more interesting than this pre-historic background is what may be called the semi-historic background which lies between it and the fairly visible, well-lighted scenery of historic time. That, too, is a discovery of our own exploring age. Half a century ago the beginnings of the most dimly known history antedated our Christian era by little more than two thousand years. Now, as the result of inquisitive digging into the sand-covered ruins of ancient cities of the East, where civilization and letters had their birth, we are reading messages from more than twice that depth in the pre-Christian past; and the story of the most ancient world has not only been extended but retold. It has been set before us in entirely new lights. In a thousand particulars, and in most of the meaning it had to modern minds, the old understanding of it is found to have been wrong. We who were read-ers of ancient history as it was written

half a century ago are having to read it
and learn it anew. The books that were
classic in this department of history a
generation ago — and they include the
books of Biblical exposition and illustra-
tion, as well as those in profane history
— are as nearly worthless to-day as hon-
est books can be made. Many readers,
I fear, are not clearly conscious of that
fact, and are wasting study on obsolete
books. The parts of history much affected
by these recent discoveries are those
which touch primitive Egypt and western Asia, and the legendary ages of the
Greeks. Otherwise, the literature of ancient history that was authoritative and
good a generation ago is so, for the most
part, now.

This reminds me to repeat a word of
counsel which I find frequent reason to
urge: Take your history, as much as
possible, from the greater writers, —
from the historians who treat it in the
largest way, with the amplest knowledge,

the most illuminating thought, the clearest style. This may seem uncalled-for advice, but it is not. In my library experience I have encountered many people who entertain a certain fear or distrust of the really great historical works. They want, as they say, something less learned, less elaborate, — something simple, comprehensive, and plain. They think it will be easier to take instruction from one volume of a compiler than from half-a-dozen of a great original work. They make a very serious mistake. The history that is " writ large," from full knowledge, is the history that can be made easy of apprehension and delightfully interesting to the mind. Those who read it in compends and compilations lose its flavors; lose the taste of life and living people in it; lose its organic wholeness, — the logic and the lesson of it; lose most, in fact, of what history is worth reading for, and do not get the simplicity and comprehensiveness they sought.

At the same time, I am convinced that it is well to prepare for the large reading of any part of history by etching into the mind, as it were, a rough outline of the whole career of the greater races of mankind, from Egypt and Babylon down to Britain and America, so that, whenever and wherever we fill in the details by fuller reading of this and that national history or individual biography, the parts will adjust themselves in their relative places and be correlated properly with each other. I do not mean by this to advise the general reader of history to cumber his mind with an extensive store of precise dates, but only that he should establish in his memory a fixed and firm association of the epochs, the important movements and the great characters that are contemporaneous, co-sequent and interactive in different regions of the world. To leave this chronological framework of historical knowledge to be pieced together as one goes on with his larger reading seems to me a mistake. Better, I should say, sit down with a good epitome and make a business of building the main sections of it into the memory at once.

It is not my purpose to commend writers or writings specifically; I am simply urging fealty to the indisputably *best*, which do not need, as a rule, to be advertised. In name, at least, they are marked generally by common fame. If they are not known they can easily be ascertained; and it is part of a reader's training to learn by sedulous inquiry what is the superlative literature in any field he may approach.

IV

THE MISSION AND THE MIS-
SIONARIES OF THE BOOK

THE MISSION AND THE MIS-
SIONARIES OF THE BOOK.[1]

FOR the most part, that lifting of the
human race in condition and character
which we call civilization has been
wrought by individual energies acting
on simply selfish lines. When I say this,
I use the term selfish in no sense that is
necessarily mean, but only as indicating
the unquestionable fact that men have
striven, in the main, each for himself more
than for one another, even in those striv-
ings that have advanced the whole race.
Within certain limits there is no discredit
to human nature in the fact. A measure
of selfishness is prescribed to man by
the terms of his individuality and the
conditions of his life. His only escape

[1] An Address at the University Convocation
(State of New York), in June, 1896.

from it is through exertions which he must employ at first in his own behalf, in order to win the independence and the power to be helpful to his fellows. So it seems to me quite impossible to imagine a process that would have worked out the civilization of the race otherwise than by the self-pushing energy that has impelled individual men to plant, to build, to trade, to explore, to experiment, to think, to plan, primarily and immediately for their own personal advantage.

But if the more active forces in civilization are mainly from selfish springs, there are two, at least, which have nobler sources and a nobler historic part. One is the sympathetic impulse which represents benevolence on its negative side, pained by the misfortunes of others and active to relieve them. In the second, which is more rare, we find benevolence of the positive kind. Its spring is in a purely generous feeling, which strongly moves one to communicate to others some good which is precious to him in his own experience of it. It is a feeling which may rise in different minds from different estimates of good, and be directed toward immediate objects that are unlike, but the disinterested motive and ultimate aim are unvarying, and it manifests in all cases the very noblest enthusiasm that humanity is capable of. There seems to be no name for it so true as that used when we speak of a missionary spirit, in efforts that aim at the sharing of some greatly cherished good with people who have not learned that it is good. At the same time we must remember that mere propagandisms put on the missionary garb without its spirit, and spuriously imitate its altruistic zeal ; and we must keep our definition in mind.

There are always true missionaries in the world, laboring with equally pure hearts, though with minds directed toward many different ends of benefaction

to their fellows. But only two objects —
the spiritual good of mankind, contemplated in religious beliefs, and the intellectual good, pursued in educational
plans — have ever wakened the missionary spirit in a large, world-moving way.
The supremely great epochs in human
history are those few which have been
marked by mighty waves of altruistic enthusiasm, sweeping over the earth from
sources of excitation found in one or the
other of these two ideals of good.

Naturally the first wakening was under
the touch of beliefs which contemplate a
more than earthly good ; and those beliefs have moved the missionary spirit at
all times with the greatest passion and
power. But even the religious wakening
was not an early event in history. I think
I may safely say that no trace of it is to
be found among the worshipers of remote
antiquity. The Hebrew prophets never
labored as dispensers of a personal blessing from their faith. It was for Israel, the

national Israel, that they preached the claims and declared the requirements of the God of Israel. The priests of Osiris and Bel were still more indifferent to the interest of the worshiper in the worship of their gods, thinking only of the honor demanded by the gods themselves. So far as history will show, the first missionary inspiration would seem to have been brought into religion by Gotama, the Buddha, whose pure and exalted but enervating gospel of renunciation filled Asia with evangelists, and was carried to all peoples as the message of a hope of deliverance from the universal sorrow of the world. Then, centuries later, came the commission more divine which sent forth the apostles of Christianity to tell the story of the Cross and to bear the offer of salvation to every human soul. As religiously kindled, the missionary spirit has never burned with more fervor than it did in the first centuries of Christian preaching; but nothing akin to it was set aflame in the smallest degree by any other eagerness of desire for the communication of a blessing or good to mankind. Until we come to modern times, I can see no mark of the missionary motive in any labor that was not religious.

The one object which, in time, as I have said, came to rival the religious object as an inspiration of missionary work, the modern zeal for education, was late and slow in moving feelings to an unselfish depth. Enthusiasm for learning at the period of the renaissance was enthusiasm among the few who craved learning, and was expended mostly within their own circle. There was little thought of pressing the good gift on the multitude who knew not their loss in the lack of it. The earliest great pleader for a common education of the whole people was Luther; but the school was chiefly important in Luther's view as the nursery of the church and as a health-bringer to the state, and he labored for it more as a means to religious and political ends than as an end in itself. Almost a century after Luther there appeared one whom Michelet has called "the first evangelist of modern pedagogy," John Amos Comenius, the Moravian. The same thought of him, as an evangelist, is expressed by the historian Raumer, who says: "Comenius is a grand and venerable figure of sorrow. Wandering, persecuted and homeless during the terrible and desolating Thirty Years' War, he yet never despaired, but with enduring truth and strong in faith he labored unweariedly to prepare youth by a better education for a better future. He labored for them with a zeal and love worthy of the chief of the Apostles." And the education for which Comenius labored was no less, in his own words, than "the teaching to all men of all the subjects of human concern." Proclaiming his educational creed at another time, he said: "I undertake an organization of schools whereby all the youth may be instructed save those to whom God has denied intelligence, and instructed in all those things which make man wise, good and holy."

Here, then, had arisen the first true missionary of common teaching, who bore the invitation to learning as a gospel proffered to all childhood and all youth, and who strove in its behalf with apostolic zeal. The period of the active labors of Comenius was before and a little after the middle of the seventeenth century. He made some impression upon the ideas and the educational methods of his time, but Europe generally was cold to his enthusiasm. In one small corner of it, alone, there was a people already prepared for and already beginning to realize his inspiring dreams of universal education. That was Holland, where the state, even in the midst of its struggle for an independent existence, was assuming the support of common schools and attempting to provide them for every

child. In that one spot the true missionary leaven in education was found working while the seventeenth century was
still young, and from Holland it would
seem to have been carried to America
long before the fermentation was really
felt in any other land.

Elsewhere in the Old World, if Comenius found any immediate successor in the
new field of missionary labor which he
had practically discovered and opened,
it was the Abbé La Salle, founder of the
great teaching order of the Christian
Brothers. But the zeal kindled by La
Salle, which has burned even to the present day, was essentially religious in its
aims and dedicated to the service of his
church. The spirit in common teaching still waited generally for that which
would make a secular saving faith of it,
urgent, persisting, not to be denied or
escaped from. The world at large made
some slow progress toward better things
in it ; schools were increased in number

and improved ; Jesuits, Jansenists, Ora-
torians and other teaching orders in
the Roman Church labored more intelli-
gently ; middle-class education in England and other countries received more
attention.   But the conscience of society
in general was satisfied with the opening of the school to those who came with
money in their hands and knocked at its
door.   There was no thought yet of standing in the door and crying out to the
moneyless and to the indifferent, bidding
them come.   Far less was there thought
of going out into the highways and
hedges to bring them in.   Another century of time was needed and a long
line of apostolic teachers, agitators, and
administrators, like Pestalozzi, Father
Girard, Fröbel, Humboldt, Brougham,
Horace Mann, to inspire that feeling for
education which warms the western na-
tions of the world at last : the feeling for
education as a supreme good in itself, not
merely as a bread-making or a money-

making instrument; not merely for giving arithmetic to the shop-keeper, or
bookkeeping to the clerk, or even political opinions to the citizen ; not merely
for supplying preachers to the pulpit, or
physicians to the sick-room, or lawyers
to the bench and bar ; but in and of and
for its own sake, as a good to humanity
which surpasses every other good, save
one. This is what I call the missionary
spirit in education, and it has so far been
wakened in the world that we expect and
demand it in the teaching work of our
time, and when we do not have it, we are
cheated by its counterfeit.

But this zeal for education was animated in most communities sooner than
the thought needed for its wise direction.
There was a time not long ago when it
expended itself in schoolrooms and colleges and was satisfied. To have laid be-
nignant hands on the children of the generation and pushed them, with a kindly
coercion, through some judicious cur-

riculum of studies was thought to be
enough. That limited conception of education as a common good sufficed for a
time, but not long. The impulse which
carried public sentiment to that length
was sure to press questions upon it that
would reach farther yet. " Have we arrived," it began to ask, "at the end for
which our public schools are the means?
We have provided broadly and liberally
— for what ? For teaching our children to
read their own language in print, to trace
it in written signs, to construct it in gram-
matical forms, to be familiar with arith-
metical rules, to know the standards and
divisions of weight and measure, to form
a notion of the surface features of the
earth and to be acquainted with the
principal names that have been given to
them, to remember a few chief facts in
the past of their own country. But these
are only keys which we expect them to
use in their acquisition of knowledge,
rather than knowledge itself. When they

quit the school with these wonderful keys of alphabet and number in their possession, they are only in the vestibule chambers of education. Can we leave them there, these children and youth of our time, to find as best they may, or not find at all, the treasuries we would have them unlock?" To ask the question was to answer it. Once challenged to a larger thought of education, the missionary spirit of the age rose boldly in its demands. The free school, the academy, the college even, grew in importance when looked at in the larger view, but they were seen to be not enough. They were seen to be only blessed openings in the way to knowledge, — garlanded gates, ivory portals, golden doors, but passage-ways only, after all, to knowledge beyond them. And the knowledge to which they led, while much and of many kinds may need to be gleaned in the open fields of life, out of living observations and experiences, yet mainly exists as a measureless store of accumulated savings from the experience and observation of all the generations that have lived and died, recorded in writing and preserved in print. There, then, in the command and possession of that great store, the end of education was seen to be most nearly realized; and so the free public library was added to the free public school.

But strangely enough, when that was first done, there happened the same halting of spirit that had appeared in the free public school. To have collected a library of books, and to have set its doors open to all comers, was assumed to be the fulfillment of duty in the matter. The books waited for readers to seek them. The librarian waited for inquirers to press their way to him. No one thought of outspreading the books of the library like a merchant's wares, to win the public eye to them. None thought of trying by any means to rouse an appetite for books in minds not naturally hungry for learning or poetry or the thinking of other men. So the free or the nearly free public libraries, for a time, wrought no great good for education beyond a circle in which the energy of the desire to which they answered was most independent of any public help.

But this stage of passive existence in the life of the free public library had no long duration. Soon the missionary passion began to stir men here and there in the library field, as it had stirred teachers in the schools before. One by one, the inspiration of their calling began to burn in their hearts. They saw with new eyes the greatness of the trust confided to them, and they rose to a new sense of the obligations borne with it. No longer a mere keeper, custodian, watchman, set over dumb treasures to hold them safe, the librarian now took active functions upon himself and became the minister of his trust, commanded by his own feelings and by many incen-

tives around him to make the most in
all possible ways of the library as an influence for good. The new spirit thus
brought into library work spread quickly,
as a beneficent epidemic, from New England, where its appearance was first no-
tably marked, over America and Great
Britain and into all English lands, and
is making its way more slowly in other
parts of the world.

The primary effort to which it urged
librarians and library trustees was that
toward bettering the introduction of
books to readers ; toward making them
known, in the first instance, with a due
setting forth of what they are and what
they offer ; then toward putting them
in right relations with one another, by
groupings according to subject and literary form and by cross-bindings of
reference ; then toward establishing the
easiest possible guidance to them, both
severally and in their groups, for all seek-
ers, whether simple or learned. When

serious attention had once been given to
these matters there was found to be need
in them of a measure of study, of experiment, of inventive ingenuity, of individual and collective experience, of practical
and philosophical attainments, that had
never been suspected before. These discoveries gave form to a conception of
"library science," of a department of
study that is entitled to scientific rank
by the importance of its results, the precision of its methods, the range of its details. The quick development of the new
science, within the few years that have
passed since the first thought of it came
into men's minds, is marked by the rise
of flourishing library schools and classes
in all parts of the United States, east and
west.

For more efficiency in their common
work, the reformers of the library were
organized at an early day. The American
Library Association on this side of the
sea and the Library Association of the

United Kingdom on the other side, with journals giving voice to each, proved powerful in their unifying effect. Ideas were exchanged and experiences compared. Each was taught by the successes or warned by the failures of his neighbors. What each one learned by investigation or proved by trial became the property of every other. The mutual instruction that came about was equaled only by the working coöperation which followed. Great tasks, beyond the power of individuals, and impossible as commercial undertakings, because promising no pecuniary reward, were planned and laboriously performed by the union of many coworkers, widely scattered in the world, but moved by one disinterested aim. From one hundred and twenty-two libraries, in that mode of alliance, there was massed the labor which indexed the whole body of general magazine literature, thus sweeping the dust from thousands of volumes that had been practically useless before, bringing the invaluable miscellany of their contents into daily, definite service, by making its subjects known and easily traced. The same work of coöperative indexing was next carried into the indeterminate field of general miscellaneous books. By still broader coöperation, a selection of books was made from the huge mass of all literature, with siftings and resiftings, to be a standard of choice and a model of cataloguing for small new libraries. And now topical lists on many subjects are being prepared for the guidance of readers by specialists in each subject, with notes to describe and value the books named. The possibilities of coöperation in library work are just beginning to be realized, and the great tasks accomplished already by it will probably look small when compared with undertakings to come hereafter.

But, after all, it is the individual work in the libraries which manifests most distinctly the new spirit of the time. The perfected cataloguing, which opens paths for the seeker from every probable starting-point of inquiry, not only to books, but into the contents of books ; the multiplied reading lists and reference lists on questions and topics of the day, which are quick to answer a momentary interest in the public mind and direct it to the best sources for its satisfaction ; the annotated bulletins of current literature, which announce and value as far as practicable, by some word of competent criticism, the more important publications of each month ; the opening of bookshelves to readers, to which libraries are tending as far as their constitution and their circumstances will permit ; the evolution of the children's reading-room, now become a standard feature to be provided for in every new building design, and to be striven for in buildings of an older pattern ; the invention of traveling libraries and home libraries ; the increasing provision made in library service for helping students and inquirers to pursue their investigations and make their searches; the increasing coöperation of libraries and schools, with the growing attraction of teachers and pupils toward the true literature of their subjects of study, and the waning tyranny of the dessicated text-book; in all these things there is the measure of an influence which was hardly beginning to be felt a quarter of a century ago.

I have named last among the fruits of this potent influence the coöperation of libraries and schools, not because it stands least in the list, but because the whole missionary inspiration from every standpoint of solicitude for the educational good of mankind is united and culminated in it and is doing its greatest work. The missionary teacher and the missionary librarian come together in these new arrangements, working no longer one in the steps of the other, — one carrying forward the education which the other has begun, — but hand in hand and side by side, leading children from the earliest age into the wonderful and beautiful book-world of poetry, legend, story, nature-knowledge, or science, time-knowledge or history, life-knowledge or biography, making it dear and familiar to them in the impressionable years within which their tastes are formed. The school alone, under common conditions, can do nothing of that. On the contrary, its text books, as known generally in the past, have been calculated to repel the young mind. They have represented to it little but the dry task of rote-learning and recitation. They have brought to it nothing of the flavor of real literature, nor any of that rapturous delight from an inner sense of rhythmic motions which real literature can give : neither the dancing step, nor the swinging march, nor the rush as with steeds, nor the lift and sweep as with wings, which even a child may be made to feel in great poetry and in noble prose, and which once experienced is a beguiling charm forever. The whole tendency of the text-book teaching of school is toward deadening the young mind to that feeling for literature, and alienating it from books by a prejudice born of wrong impressions at the beginning. Just so far as the school reader, the school geography, the school history and their fellow compends, are permitted to remain conspicuous in a child's thought during his early years, as representative of the books which he will be admonished by and by to read, so far he will be put into an opposition never easy to overcome.

The tenderest years of childhood are the years of all others for shaping a pure intellectual taste and creating a pure intellectual thirst which only a noble literature can satisfy in the end. We have come at last to the discernment of that pregnant fact, and our schemes of education for the young are being reconstructed accordingly. There is no longer the division of labor between school and library which seemed but a little time ago to be marked out so plainly. Schools are not to make readers for libraries, nor are libraries to wait for readers to come to them out of the schools. The school and the world of books which it makes known to him are to be identified in the child's mind. There is to be no distinction in his memory between reading as an art learned and reading as a delight discovered. The art and the use of the art are to be one simultaneous communication to him.

That is the end contemplated in the coöperative work of libraries and schools, which, recent in its beginning, has made great advances already, and which especially appeals to what I have called the missionary enthusiasm in both libraries and schools. It contemplates what seems to be the truest ideal of teaching ever shaped in thought: of teaching not as educating, but as setting the young in the way of education; as starting them on a course of self-culture which they will pursue to the end of their lives, with no willingness to turn back. The highest ideal of education is realized in that life-long pursuit of it, and the success of any school is measured, not by the little portion of actual learning which its students take out of it, but by the persisting strength of the impulse to know and to think, which they carry from the school into their later lives.

But there are people who may assent to all that is said of education in this life-lasting view of it, who will deny that there is a question in it of books. "We," they say, "find more for our instruction in life than in books. The reality of things interests us more and teaches us more than the report and description of them by others. We study men among men and God's works in the midst of them. We prefer to take knowledge at first hand, from nature and from society, rather than second-handedly, out of a printed page. Your book-wisdom is from the closet and for closet-use. It is not the kind needed in a busy and breezy world." Well, there is a half-truth in this which must not be ignored. To make everything of books in the development of men and women is a greater mistake, perhaps, than to make nothing of them. For life has teachings, and nature out of doors has teachings, for which no man, if he misses them, can find compensation in books. We can say that frankly to the contemner of books and we yield no ground in doing so; for then we turn upon him and say: " Your life, sir, to which you look for all the enlightenment of soul and mind that you receive, is a brief span of a few tens of years; the circle of human acquaintances in which you are satisfied to make your whole study of mankind is a little company of a few hundred men and women, at the most; the natural world from which you think to take sufficient lessons with your unassisted eyes is made up of some few bits of city streets and country lanes and seaside sands. What can you, sir, know of life, compared with the man who has had equal years of breath and consciousness with you, and who puts with that experience some large, wide knowledge of seventy centuries of human history in the whole round world besides? What can you know of mankind and human nature compared with the man who meets and talks with as many of his neighbors in the flesh as yourself, and who, beyond that, has companionship and communion of mind with the kingly and queenly ones of all the generations that are dead? What can you learn from nature compared with him who has Darwin and Dana and Huxley and Tyndall and Gray for his tutors when he walks abroad, and who, besides the home-rambling which he shares with you, can go bird-watching with John

Burroughs up and down the Atlantic states, or roaming with Thoreau in Maine woods, or strolling with Richard Jefferies in English lanes and fields?"

Truth is, the bookless man does not understand his own loss. He does not know the leanness in which his mind is kept by want of the food which he rejects. He does not know what starving of imagination and of thought he has inflicted upon himself. He has suffered his interest in the things which make up God's knowable universe to shrink until it reaches no farther than his eyes can see and his ears can hear. The books which he scorns are the telescopes and reflectors and reverberators of our intellectual life, holding in themselves a hundred magical powers for the overcoming of space and time, and for giving the range of knowledge which belongs to a really cultivated mind. There is no equal substitute for them. There is nothing else which will so break for us the poor hobble of every-day sights and sounds and habits and tasks, by which our thinking and feeling are prone to be tethered to a little worn round.

Some may think, perhaps, that newspapers should be named with books as sharing this high office. In truth, it ought to be possible to rank the newspaper with the book as an instrument of culture. Equally in truth, it is not possible to do so, except in the case of some small number. The true public journal — diary of the world — which is actually a *news*-paper and not a *gossip*-paper, is most powerfully an educator, cultivator, broadener of the minds of those who read it. It lifts them out of their petty personal surroundings, and sets them in the midst of all the great movements of the time on every continent. It makes them spectators and judges of everything that happens or is done, demands opinions from them, extorts their sympathy and moves them morally to wrath or admiration. In a word, it produces daily, in their thought and feeling, a thousand large relations with their fellow men of every country and race, with noble results of the highest and truest cultivation.

But the common so-called newspaper of the present day, which is a mere rag-picker of scandal and gossip, searching the gutters and garbage-barrels of the whole earth for every tainted and unclean scrap of personal misdoing or mishap that can be dragged to light; the so-called newspaper which interests itself, and which labors to interest its readers, in the trivialities and ignoble occurrences of the day — in the prize fights, and mean preliminaries of prize fights, the boxing matches, the ball games, the races, the teas, the luncheons, the receptions, the dresses, the goings and comings and private doings of private persons — making the most in all possible ways of all petty things and low things, while

treating grave matters with levity and
impertinence, with what effect is such
a newspaper read? I do not care to
say. If I spoke my mind I might strike
harshly at too many people whose reading is confined to such sheets. I will
venture only so much remark as this:
that I would prefer absolute illiteracy
for a son or daughter of mine, total in-
ability to spell a printed word, rather
than that he or she should be habitually
a reader of the common newspapers of
America to-day, and a reader of nothing
better.

I could say the same of many books.
So far, in speaking of books, I have been
taking for granted that you will understand me to mean, not everything without discrimination which has the form of
a book, but only the true literature which
worthily bears that printed form. For if
we must give the name to all printed
sheets, folded and stitched together in a
certain mode, then it becomes necessary

to qualify the use we make of the name.
Then we must sweep out of the question
vast numbers of books which belong to
literature no more than a counterfeit
dollar belongs to the money of the country. They are counterfeits in literature,
— base imitations of the true book; that
is their real character. Readers may be
cheated by them precisely as buyers and
sellers may be cheated by the spurious
coin, and the detection and rejection of
them are effected by identically the same
process of scrutiny and comparison.
Every genuine book has a reason for its
existence, in something of value which it
brings to the reader. That something
may be information, it may be in ideas,
it may be in moral stimulations, it may be
in wholesome emotions, it may be in gifts
to the imagination, or to the fancy, or to
the sense of humor, or to the humane
sympathies, or indefinably to the whole
conscious contentment of the absorbing
mind ; but it will always be a fact which

those who make themselves familiar with good and true books can never mistake. Whether they find it in a book of history, or of travel, or of biography, or of piety, or of science, or of poetry, or of nonsense (for there are good books of nonsense, like "Alice in Wonderland," for example), they will infallibly recognize the stamp of genuineness upon it. The readers who are cheated by base and worthless books are the readers who will not give themselves an expert knowledge of good books, as they might easily do.

Here, then, opens one of the greater missionary fields of the public library. To push the competition of good books against worthless books, making readers of what is vulgar and flat acquainted with what is wholesome and fine, is a work as important as the introduction of books among people who have never read at all. There is a theory which has some acceptance, that *any* reading is better than *no* reading. It rests on the assumption that an appetite for letters once created, even by the trash of the press, will either refine its own taste or else will have prepared a susceptibility to literary influences which could not otherwise exist. Those who hold this doctrine have confidence that a young devourer of dime novels, for example, may be led on an ascending plane through Castlemon, Optic, Alger, Mayne Reid, Henty, Verne, Andersen, De Foe, Scott, Homer, Shakspere, more easily than a boy or girl who runs away from print of every sort can be won into any similar path. For my own part, I fear the theory is unsafe for working. It will probably prove true in some cases; I am quite sure that it will prove dangerously false in many others. There are kinds of habit and appetite in reading which seem to be as deep-rooted in unhealthy states of mind and brain as the appetite for opium or alcohol. They grow up among the habitual readers of such newspapers as I have been speaking of, and equally among readers of the slop-shop novels, vulgar or vile, with which the world is flooded in this age of print. The newspaper appetite or the trash-novel appetite, once fastened on the brain of its victim, is not often unloosed. It masters all other inclinations, permits no other taste or interest to be wakened. The stuff which produces it is as dangerous to tamper with as any other dream- and stupor-making narcotic. To bait readers with it, expecting to lure them on to better literature, is to run a grave risk of missing the end and realizing only the mischiefs of the temptation.

Far safer will it be to hold the public library as strictly as can be done to the mission of good books. And that is a vague prescription. How are "good books" to be defined?—since their goodness is of many degrees. The mere distinction between good and bad in literature I believe to be recognized easily, as I have said, by every person who has tasted the good and whose intellectual sense has been cultivated by it to even a small extent. But between the supremely good and that which is simply not bad, there are degrees beyond counting. From Sardou to Shakspere, from Trumbull to Homer, from Roe to Thackeray, from Tupper to Marcus Aurelius, from Talmage to Thomas à Kempis or Thomas Fuller, from Jacob Abbott to Edward Gibbon, the graduation of quality is beyond exact marking by any critical science. How shall we draw lines to distinguish the negatively from the positively good in letters? We simply cannot. We can only lay down loose lines and put behind them the never relaxing spring of one elastic and always practicable rule: Strive unceasingly for the best. Give all the opportunities to the best literature of every class. Give front places on all possible occasions to the great writers, the wise writers, the learned writers, the wholesome writers; keep them always in evidence; contrive introductions for them; make readers familiar with their standing and rank. There is little else to be done. The public library would be false to its mission if it did not exclude books that are positively bad, either through vice or vulgarity; but much beyond that it cannot easily go. Happily, it cannot force the best literature upon its public; for if it could, the effect would be lost. But it can recommend the best, with an insisting urgency that will prevail in the end.

I am by nature an optimist. Things as they are in the world look extremely disheartening to me, but I think I can see forces at work which will powerfully change them before many generations have passed. Among such forces, the most potent in my expectation is that which acts from the free public library.

Through its agency, in my belief, there will come a day — it may be a distant day, but it will come — when the large knowledge, the wise thinking, the fine feeling, the amplitude of spirit that are in the greater literatures, will have passed into so many minds that they will rule society democratically, by right of numbers. I see no encouragement to hope that the culture which lifts men from generation to generation, little by little, to higher levels and larger visions of things, will ever be made universal. Under the best circumstances which men can bring about, nature seems likely to deny to a considerable class of unfortunates the capacity, either mentally, or morally, or both, for refinement and elevation. But if that be true at all, it cannot be true of any formidable number. Among the progressive races, the majority of men and women are unquestionably of the stuff and temper out of which anything fine in soul and strong in intellect can be made, if not in one generation, then in two, or three, or ten, by the continual play upon them of influences from the finer souls and greater minds of their own times and of the past. It is not by nature but by circumstance, heredity itself being an offspring of circumstance, that light is shut from the greater part of those who walk the earth with darkened minds. Man is so far the master of circumstance that he can turn and diffuse the light almost as he will, and his will to make the illumination of the few common to the many is now beyond dispute. All the movements that I have reviewed are marks of its progressive working. It translates into active energy that desire for others of the good most precious to one's self, which is the finest and noblest feeling possible to human nature. All the forces of selfishness that race men against one another, from goal to goal of a simply scientific civilization, would fail to bring about this supreme end of a common culture for the race. Nothing but the missionary inspiration could give a reasonable promise of it. Let us thank God for the souls He has put into men, having that capability of helpfulness to one another.

V

GOOD AND EVIL FROM THE PRINTING PRESS

GOOD AND EVIL FROM THE PRINTING PRESS [1]

FROM the first movement of its lever, the Press brought an immeasurable new force into modern civilization. Its earliest service was rendered mainly to scholarship, in the diffusion of the classic writings of antiquity, but very quickly it was drawn into a more popular arena, and gave a voice to the appeals of religion, a weapon to theological dispute. The rapidity of its work at that early period is shown by the rapidity of the spread of the ideas of the Reformation, for which it was a vehicle that could not have been spared. Between Gutenberg's death and Luther's birth there were only fifteen

[1] From an address at the meeting of the American Library Association, 1896.

years ; but the reformer found already an extensive public prepared to be reached and acted on by the printed tract and book. That the intellectual horizons of life were widened from that day is one of the plainest historical facts. Its skies, too, were lifted to a loftier arch, and it was made larger in all ways, by energies which the new instrument of knowledge set free. For then, and long afterward, there was earnestness in the splendid work of type and press. Some kind of purpose — not always good, or wise, or true, or wholesome, but something that had thought behind it, or fact, or imagination, or emotion, — was in most things that received the printer's stamp. Through the sixteenth, seventeenth, and eighteenth centuries there are not many shallows in the stream of print.

At the opening of the nineteenth century the book and the tract remained still the principal products of the Press, and the custody or conveyance of ideas was still its chief employ. It had engaged itself already in a lighter service, as the messenger of news ; but that was a mere apprenticeship, not yet promising of much effect. So long as the gathering of news depended on the vehicles of the olden time, it was too slow and too limited a work to stir the world. But when the energy of steam and the speed of lightning were offered to the Newspaper Press, that passed suddenly to the front of all the influences acting on mankind. School, pulpit, and platform were left behind it. The mastery of our later civilization, in the moral moulding of it, if not more, was soon seen to have been grasped by adventurers in a new commerce, which made merchandise of passing history and marketed the tidings of the day.

Meantime, the common school had been doing its work far and wide, and most men and women of the leading races had learned to read. That is to say,

they had learned to decipher language
put into print, or had learned reading as
a simple art; but the educational use —
the culture use — of the art was something which no majority of them had yet
acquired. To make readers of them
practically as well as potentially, another
agency was wanted beyond that of the
school, and the newspaper came appar-
ently to supply it. Books and libraries
of books were not equal to the service
required. Perhaps it will always be impossible for book literature of any kind
to push its way or to be pushed into the
hands of the people with the penetrating
energy that carries newspapers to all
homes. At all events, the common school,
making possible readers, and the newspaper inviting them to read, arrived
together, at a conjunction which might
have seemed to be a happy miracle for
the universalizing of culture in the
Western world. The opportunity that
came then into the hands of the conductors

of the news press, with the new powers that had been given them, has never been paralleled in human history. They might have been gardeners of Eden and planters of a new paradise on the earth; for its civilization was put into their hands to be made what they would have it to be. If it could have been possible then to deal with newspapers as other educational agencies are dealt with; to invest them with definite moral responsibilities to the public; to take away from them their commercial origin and their mercenary motive; to inspire them with disinterested aims; to endow them as colleges are endowed; to man them for their work as colleges are manned, with learning and tried capacity in the editorial chairs; — if that could have been possible, what imaginable degree of common culture might not Europe and America be approaching to-day? As it is, we are trying to explain to ourselves a condition of society which alarms and shames all who think of it.

Nevertheless, during the first few decades of the modern news market, — as it took shape, we will say, early in the eighteen-forties, — the influence of the newspapers was generally more wholesome than otherwise. Readers of them were made acquainted with things worth the knowing. The world and their life in it, as parts of a great whole, were widened to them wholesomely and genuinely, and by much more than the larger knowledge of it which they gathered from day to day. The widening of the sympathetic life of mankind, meaning thereby an increment and expansion of all the feelings which press men into closer and warmer relations, and prepare them for truer understandings of each other, was the supreme effect upon them of the daily world-history that began to be reported to them in the period named.

But a time came when one arose among the brokers of the news market who made a discovery which proved nearly fatal to the character and dignity of journalism. He discerned, that is, with low shrewdness, an unbounded possibility of degradation in human curiosity and vanity, as opening a great, vulgar, and profitable field for unscrupulous exploitations of the newspaper press. He was not long alone in the enjoyment of his ignoble discovery. One by one, the traffickers in news yielded to the corrupting example, or were driven by less scrupulous competitors into the ranks of the new journalism; till, to-day, we can count on the fingers of not many hands the important newspapers (in America, at least) that will give us real and clean news, and not force us to strain some meagre pickings of it out of a sickening mixture of trivialities, morbidities, vulgarities, impertinences, and worse.

Here and there we may still bow with respect before a newspaper over which the responsible editor has kept his sovereignty. In most instances he has been deposed, and the irresponsible reporter reigns in his place, — master of the awful power of the Press, — chief educator of his generation, — pervading genius of the civilization of his time. Trained to look at all things, in heaven above or in the earth beneath, with an eye single to the glory of big type, he sees them in one aspect. The great and the little, the good and the bad, the sweet and the foul, the momentous and the trivial, the tragic and the comic, the public and the sacredly private, are of one stuff in his eyes, — mere colorings of a fabric of life which Time weaves for him to slit and to slash with his merciless, indifferent shears. And so, with little prejudice and small partiality between things high and low, he makes the daily literature on which most of us feed and tincture our minds. It is a monotoned literature, and its one note is flippancy: the flippant headline, the flippant paragraph, the flip-

pant narrative, the flippant comment. To
jest at calamity, to be jocular with crime,
to sting personal misfortune with a smart
impertinence or cap it with a slang
phrase; to be respectful and serious toward nothing else so much as toward the
gayeties of the world of fashion and the
gaming of the world of sport, appear to
be the perfections of the art to which he
is trained.

And no careful observer can fail to see
that the degradation of the newspaper
press is degrading most of the voices of
the time. The shallow flippancy which
began in journalism is affecting literature in every popular form. More and
more the air is filled with thin strains
of wordy song; but the deep-toned mel-
odies of thoughtful poetry are dying
out of it fast. Rhymers multiply apace,
and the reporter inspires them. They
worship the god Novelty with him, and
Apollo is forgotten. They exercise a
nimble fancy on tight-ropes and trapezes

of metrical invention, in performances that are curious to behold.

The art-world, too, is infected with the irresponsible levity which had its genesis in the newspaper. Half of the men and women who paint pictures are doing so with scornful denials of any thoughtful purpose in their work. " Art for Art's sake " is the senseless formula of their contempt for the reverent service of imagination and reason which Art could command from them if Art knew them at all.

On all the commoner sides of its life there is singularly and lamentably a shallowness, a flippancy, a vulgarity, in the present age. Who can dispute the fact? And what is plainer than the causes we can find, in that precipitate, enormous expansion and acceleration of communication in the world which has occurred within our time, acting on civilized society, and most powerfully in America, in three modes, namely: (1) an increas-

ing excitement of commerce, following
closely upon the loss from it of all its
older incidents of discovery and adventure, producing, for the time, a vulgariz-
ing mercenary nakedness ; (2) an abrupt
plunge for the freer peoples from theo-
retical into practical democracy, consequent on the sudden creation of tremendous new agencies of combination and
organization, and the generating of a
public opinion that is a new and untrained
force in the world ; (3) the evolution of
the modern newspaper and its speedy
corruption, from the mighty servant of
civilization that it ought to be into the
busy pander of every vulgarity that the
new conditions can feed.

But this is not the end of the story.
These are but early effects, — effects in
their beginning, from great enduring
causes, the operation of which they cannot exhaust. If the common mind of the
age is trivialized and vulgarized by its
newspapers and its commerce, it is being

pricked, at the same time, to a new alertness, even by the worst journalism and the fiercest money-making, and faculties are being wakened in it that will some day answer the call to higher uses. The influences which will bear on it to that result are gathering volume and weight. For powerful forces are working even now in the world to broaden life for those who will have it so, not superficially, but profoundly, and not in mere sense and circumstance, but in consciousness and power.

There are some ideas which, when they have got a setting in the mind, are like magnifying lenses to the eye of reason, clearing and enlarging its whole vision of things. The Copernican idea of the structure of the universe was such an one. By dispelling the human egotism of the view which put man and his habitation at the centre of creation, it opened new vistas to thinking in a hundred directions. The idea which Newton brought to light, of a unity of law in the universe, was another. The completer development of that idea in the doctrine of the correlation of forces, or the present notion of energy, is another. But of all the emancipating conceptions which, one by one, have entered and possessed the mind of man, there was never one before that brought such liberations with it as came in Darwin's message to our own time. It is hardly too much to say that the full, free exercise of human reason on all the greater problems of life and destiny, whether personal or social, really began with the perception and apprehension of evolutionary processes in God's work. That has raised the thinking minds of our day to a summit of observation which was never attainable before, while eager science brings daily new helps to them for the expansion of their view.

It is true that this intellectual expansion of life is known nowhere to all men. Even so much of it as goes with vague glimpses of the working of universal law is still no common experience; while those who know it in its fullness are everywhere a few. But something from it is diffusing itself in the whole atmosphere of the age; something penetrating, stimulating, virile; something which most men are compelled to feel whether they comprehend it or not, and to which the finer elements in them must respond by some sort of rally and growth. Of hopeful phenomena in the world, that one is the greatest of all. It indexes a new state of the common mind, now cleared for the most part of old superstitions, and thus prepared for the receiving of light to dispel its old ignorances.

And what a wakening of moral no less than intellectual energies there is in our time, for work directed to that end! A little while ago the steam engine, the factory, the forge, the mine, the mart, represented about all the human energy that made itself conspicuous in the civilized world, excepting some occasional explosions of it in movements of religious and political enthusiasm and in raging outbursts of war. To-day it is not so. No little part of the interest, the ardor, the force, the ingenuity which spent themselves on those objects before are going over into a very different field. We are seeing the rise of an enterprise in education which almost rivals the enterprise of mechanic industry and trade. Invention is half as busy in the improving of schools, in the perfecting of instruction, in the circulating of books, in the stimulating of reading and study, as it used to be busy in the making of machines. The diffusion of literature is left no longer to depend, like the diffusion of cotton fabrics or tea, on the mercenary agencies of trade. Half a century ago the free public library was created. For thirty years past it has been worked over by one set of people, just as the steam engine has been worked over by another set, and the electric dynamo by a third. Its powers have been learned, its efficiency developed, in the same scientific way. Cunning variations of form are being wrought in it, to fit all circumstances and to do its civilizing work in all places. It becomes a Traveling Library to make its way into villages and rural corners of the land. It becomes a Home Library to reach the tenement-houses and purlieus of the city. It spreads itself in branches and delivery stations. It distributes choice reading in the schools, to broaden the teacher's work. It drums and advertises its unpriced wares like a shop-keeper, avaricious of gain. It is taking up the eager, laborious, strenuous spirit of the present age, and wresting some large part of it away from the sordid activities of life, to give it unmercenary aims.

So books are being made to do considerably alone what books and newspapers ought rightly to be doing together.

As a carrier in the spiritual commerce of the world, the book is not nearly so agile, so lightly winged, so Mercury-like as the newspaper can be; but when each is at the best, how much nobler is the freightage of books!

I rest my faith in a future of finer culture for mankind on the energy of free public libraries in distributing good books, far more than on any other agency that is working in the world. So far they have but opened gates into the field of influence that is before them; but the gates are really swung wide, and the length and breadth of the field is fully seen, and the spirit that will possess it and work in it is eagerly alive. I speak soberly when I say that the greatest antagonism to be met and overcome is that of the vulgarized part of the newspaper press. I say this with persisting iteration, because I am convinced that it is the fact which needs most at the present day to be understood. How to win readers of

the general mass from unwholesome
newspapers to wholesome books, or how
to change the spirit of the common newspapers of the day from flippancy to so-
briety, — from the tone of the worst in
social manners and morals to the tone of
the best, — is one of the gravest pending
problems of civilization, if not the gravest
of all. The zeal and energy of free schools
and free libraries can achieve the solu-
tion of it, and I see nothing else that can.

VI

PUBLIC LIBRARIES AND
PUBLIC EDUCATION

PUBLIC LIBRARIES AND PUBLIC EDUCATION [1]

THE function of our free circulating libraries is *diffusion*, which is a function of active responsibility. The prime purpose of their institution is to bring to bear upon the greatest possible number of people the profitable influences that are found in books. That object restricts them to no narrow range. It takes in whatever can be tributary to all that has excellence and value in men. It embraces the wholesome literature of imagination and emotion, no less than the literature of knowledge and thought. The graces and harmonies of education, and the sweetenings and colorings of life, are compre-

[1] From a paper read before the American Social Science Association, in 1883.

hended equally with the ethics and the practical powers. There is no narrowness in the range, as I have said; but it has a well-marked bound. It is bounded by all the lines in literature which separate purity from grossness, art from rubbish, good from bad. It is so bounded by its purpose, which I think I have stated with precision when I say that the sole reason for the existence of a popular library is the endeavor made through it to bring to bear on the greatest possible number of people the profitable influences that are in books; and it has no excuse for being if it cannot discriminate with some success between the profitable and the unprofitable quality of books.

Of course this involves a selective criticism, or a censorship of books, if one chooses to call it so, in the government of popular libraries; but what then? Is not the same kind of selective criticism, — the same kind of discriminative judgment, — the same censorial assumption,

— involved in all public services, from legislation down? To what public institution will it be denied? If a gallery of art is founded, for the finer teaching of the eyes of the people, and for kindling the light of the love of beauty in their souls, does any one claim a place in it for the pictorial advertisements of the circus, or for the popular sculpture of the cemeteries, on the ground that there is a public which finds pleasure in them? Yet something comparable with that demand is found in the frequent expectation that public libraries shall descend to levels of taste in literature which all cultivated taste condemns. It is assumed quite naturally that somewhere in the control of a public art-collection there shall be an instructed criticism at work, to distinguish, with what care and capability it can, the true productions of art from its counterfeits, and to set up certain standards of taste which it is desirable to have urged upon the public for common recognition. Wherein are the considerations which bear on the popularizing of literature and the teaching of books, by means of public libraries, different from those that bear on the popularizing of art by public museums of painting, sculpture, and design? If they differ at all it is by reason of the greater power and greater importance of the educating influence in books.

I am not thinking altogether of questions touching fiction in public libraries, which have been much discussed; though that, in the treatment of this subject, takes, of course, the foremost place. It is a question much discussed, but not always on broad grounds. Here is a form of literature that we have seen, almost in our own generation, rise from a modest rank in the realm of letters to undisputed ascendency. It has introduced a new Muse to our Olympus and has throned her royally in the highest seat, where the crown and the sceptre, the honors and the powers of the pen, are alike given up to her. For my part, I am submissive to the revolution that has brought us under this new reign in literature; I have no discontent with it. I recognize the modern Romance, or Novel, as the true heir and natural successor of the Epic and the Drama, which held anciently, in their turn, the regal place in literature. I look upon it as representing no mere literary fashion of the day, but distinctly a development in literary art — the plastic shaping by organic growth of a new, perfected form of epic and dramatic expression moulded in one; fitting itself to new conditions of general culture, with more versatile capabilities and powers. It is not alone approved by the suffrages of the multitude, it is preferred by the bards and "makers" themselves. More and more we can see that the dramatic genius of the age turns lovingly to this new form of art and expends itself upon it. If Shakspere were living in these days, I doubt not we should have more novels than plays from his pen.

At all events the chief power in literature for our generation belongs to the novel, and if we will recognize and deal with it broadly in that view there is nothing lamentable in the fact. Let us freely concede to it the great domain it has won for itself on the art-side of literature, and pay to it the respect we give to all art — no less, no more. We can hardly claim to have done that yet. There is something half disdainful, half shamed and apologetic, in the very homage conceded to this new-comer among the Muses. Her devotees do not seem to be quite assured of her Olympian reputability, and find, perhaps, a little pleasure in the suspicion that she and Folly are near kin. So we all continue to speak of the realm of "light literature;" as though the literature that is weighted with the fruits of the genius of George Eliot, Thackeray, Dickens, Balzac, Hawthorne,

Scott, De Foe, can justly be called "light."
The *lightness* which it has is the lightness
of the spirit of art — the lightness which
art takes from the up-bearing wings on
which it is exalted, and whereby it has
the power to transport us high and far,
and make us travelers beyond the swim-
ming of ships or the rolling of wheels.

Whatever it may be that acts on men
with that kind of power is a factor in
education as important as science or history. It is like the wine and sweetness
of the fruits which are the wholesome
peptic trifles of our bodily food, and
it contributes quite as much as the
strong meats of learning to a vigorous
and symmetrical growth of human character. In the novel, these potencies of
art are universalized more than in any
preceding form; it brings a larger mass
of mankind within their range, to be
quickened in spirit by them and to be
wrought upon by an inward leaven which
human beings are sodden without. As

a true product of art in literature, the novel seems to me to be a great instrument of education, in the large sense of the word — not for all men and women, perhaps, but for most, and especially for those whose lives are narrow and constrained. There are not many of us who do not owe to it some reaches and happy vistas of the intellectual landscape in which we live, and the compass of our thoughts, feelings, sympathies, tolerances, would shrink sadly if they were taken away. It is only a little region of actual things that we can include in our personal horizons — a few individual people, a few communities, a few groups and growths of society, a few places, a few situations and arrangements of circumstance, a few movements of events, that we can know and be familiar with by any intimacy and experience of our own. But how easily our neighborhoods and acquaintances are multiplied for us by the hospitable genius of the novelist ! To be put in companionship with Caleb Garth and Adam Bede, with Colonel Newcome and Henry Esmond; to meet Mrs. Poyser and Mr. Weller; to visit in Barsetshire with Mr. Trollope and loiter through Alsace with the Messrs. Erckmann and Chatrian; to look on Saxon England with the imagination of Kingsley, on Eighteenth-century England with the sympathetic understanding of Thackeray, on Puritan Massachusetts with the clairvoyance of Hawthorne — how large and many-sided a life must be to embrace in its actualities so much of a ripening education as this!

But, if there is no other form in which the broadening influences of art can be exercised more powerfully than in the novel, there is no other form that lends itself to base counterfeiting so easily. And the vulgar product is vulgar beyond comparison with any other. More than vulgar; for the travesty of life which these romances of book-smithing exhibit is mischievous in its whole effect. Every feeling that they act upon, every sentiment that they stimulate, every idea that they produce, is infected with the falsity that is in them. Neither virtue nor piety in the intention with which they are composed can better very much the evil influence they exert; for clean as they may be of all other vice, there is wickedness in their misrepresentations and depravity in their untruth. I see nothing for my own part but malarial unwholesomeness, breeding moral distempers and intellectual debility, in the trash of fiction with which the world is being flooded, whether it emanates from the " Satanic " or the Sunday-School press.

No agency is available for resisting this flood so effectively and so responsibly as the public library. I do not know that its right to exercise upon literature the criticism which discriminates art from rubbish is ever disclaimed formally, but it seems often to stand in some doubt.

Perhaps the criticism demanded in this case is not distinguished clearly from the presuming and very different censorship that would inspect opinions, and undertake to judge for the public between true and false teaching in religion, or politics, or social economy; but the two have no principle in common. They differ as the insolence of sumptuary laws differs from the sound reasonableness of laws for the suppression of counterfeits and adulterations. If there could be an institution for the purveying of food, or drugs, or any kind of material provision, that should stand in a relation to the public like that of the free library, we would certainly deny its right to a jurisdiction over the demands of the people so far as concerned the kinds and varieties of commodities to be supplied; but just as certainly we would hold it responsible for the *quality* of the things it had been instituted to provide. We would reasonably require the institution to be so organized as to embrace within its management the capability to distinguish competent from incompetent work, and genuine from counterfeited products. That is precisely the kind of discrimination to be exercised in public libraries in the matter of this romance literature, which is worth so much as a product of literary art and is so worthless when wanting the touches of art. The question concerning it is almost purely a question of quality. Where a subtler question arises, — a debatable question of taste, within the range of uncertain canons in which questions of taste are open, — I would not ask to have it arbitrated in a public library. But the great mass of the trash of fiction is not touched by such questions. The discernment of its worthlessness depends on nothing but some familiar acquaintance with good literature, and on the sense of quality which that acquaintance will develop.

If public libraries do no more than

administer those common verdicts of the literary world that are of authority and weight, they will sweep a mountain of rubbish from their shelves; they will command from the public a hearing for criticism that will never be secured otherwise, and they will be exercising in a most important particular the educational responsibility that belongs to them. The safe rule under which I should like to see them placed in their dealing with romance is the rule of conservatism — of slowness — of waiting for the judgments and verdicts by which literary work is proved. They are not speculators in the book market; their interest in literature is not a commercial one, like Mudie's; they are instituted for a missionary purpose, and their business, as I have said, is to bring to bear on the greatest number of people the profitable influences that are in books. Why should they be in haste to catch up the novelties of the romance press, like merchants eager for

custom? Why should they not keep all
this doubtful literature waiting at their
doors till it has been weighed and pro-
nounced upon, not by the public opinion
of Tom, Dick and Harry, and the school-
girls, and the idle and raw-minded body
of readers, but by the instructed public
opinion which is the court of last resort
for all books, and which determines the
ultimate fate of all?

I have not touched the question of
morals as affecting this literature, because
that is included substantially in the question of literary *quality*. In America and
England (I say nothing of other countries) the literary taste which prevails and
has authority is moral enough, because
healthy enough, to be trusted fairly with
the whole adjudication. I know of no
vicious or unwholesome novel, poem,
play, or other imaginative work belong-
ing to contemporary literature, that has
standing enough in the English-speaking
literary world to commend it to a public

library, if nothing is considered but the view of it from literary standpoints. Generally, I think, among the Teutonic peoples, the conception of art is essentially a moral conception, — the conception of a fundamental purity, — and the more highly the art-sense of these peoples is cultivated the more clear-sighted it becomes as to the falsity in art of all moral falsity. And so I should feel safe in making it the rule for public libraries of the popular class, that they should admit freely whatever wins a good standing in the literary public opinion of the time, and admit nothing till that standing is assured to it.

There is a large body of older literature which requires some different rule. It comes to us from coarse or corrupted periods of the past, when the ethics of literary art were slightly perceived, little felt. In some of it there are all the admirable qualities that imaginative literature produced without moral sensitiveness can have. It is vigorous, brilliant, graceful. It gained in its own day a literary standing which it could not win in ours; but we are disposed, and perhaps rightly, to let it stand at the original rating. Historically, as representative literature, it has great importance and interest to those who will use it in that character, as students of literature and history in the thorough-going sense. But I can see no good purpose it can serve in popular libraries, and no reason for its having a place in them. The drama of the Restoration, a great part of the more famous novels of the eighteenth century, with much of the older romance, are examples of what I mean. On what reasonable ground is acquaintance with them popularized at the present day? Of the kindred literature from other languages that has been imported into the English by translation, I can only ask the same question with more emphasis.

I leave large ranges of literature, in

which nothing I have said will offer a hint of the bounds I am asking to have set for our popular libraries ; and I am ready to confess with frankness that I do not know where to set the bounds, nor how. Perhaps it is not a practicable thing to do. And yet I am sure the attempt should be made to mark out, in all literature, with some rough consistency, the provinces of the popular library, as distinguished from the library of research and history, or the museum of books. Not, I say again, to set narrow or parsimonious limitations upon them. It is no petty conception of the popular library that I have formed. For popular uses I want it as great as it can be made. Not for uses of common reading only, but for all uses. I should have looked but a little way into the influence of these libraries if I took account of no more than the set "reading" that they encourage and supply. They have a greater office than that. It is to induce a habit among people of following up the chance topics and questions in which their interest happens from time to time to be stirred by casual circumstances and hints. A school exercise, a newspaper paragraph, an allusion from the pulpit, a picture, a quotation, a play, will often supply an impulse that carries itself long and far into the intellectual life and growth of our library students, but which, without the help of the public library, would come to naught. Making it common and habitual, in some wide circle of people, to say on such occasions, "I will go to the library and pursue this matter," or "put this statement to the proof," or "learn more of this man" or "of these writings," the public library brings into action more energies of education than can be organized in any college or school. And so, for its greatest efficiency, it needs to be equipped largely, liberally, with resources for every kind of common investigation ; for every kind of investigation, I mean, that is not elaborated in professional study, or special scientific research, or minute erudition. For such special quests and profounder pursuits of learning I do not think that the popular library should undertake the providing of books. All the resources it can command will seldom be too great for employment in its own great office, which is to popularize the profitable influence of books.

Before everything else it should have these two aims: First, to be abounding in its supply of good literature, within the range of popular use; second, to be perfect in arrangements for exhibiting its stores and making them accessible, and to be fertile and persistent in devices for winning students and for helping them with all encouraging aids. If the library is stinted anywhere, let it not be in the better books for which there is most of a popular call. Better fifty copies of one book that will get so many readers, than

fifty various books which few will use. I
am disposed to believe that a popular
library should expend its means very
grudgingly upon wider acquisitions until
it has so multiplied on its shelves the few
best books most wanted by its general
readers that it will seldom disappoint a
call for one of them. I put that forward
as the first claim upon its funds ; and next
to that I put the employment of adequate
methods for exhibiting and advertising
its books and their contents and character to the public. Classification, annota-
tion, analysis, in catalogues and bulletins, with indexes, reference-lists, helpful
hand-books, and bibliographical guides,
— these are objects of expenditure more
important than the gathering of numer-
ous books. A small, well-chosen library,
in systematic order, opening every ave-
nue to its contents that can be cleared
and lighted up by judicious labor, — inspiring, leading, and helping its studious
readers by all the methods which the

earnest library workers of this country
are learning to employ, — is an agent of
education more powerful than the greatest collection can ever become, if the
ambition in the latter to *have* books out-
runs the ambition to spread the influence of its books. Both of these ambitions
are working, more or less, in the popular
libraries of this country ; but the spirit of
the time and the race is on the side of
the wiser purpose, and it is wonderful to
see with what contagion of zeal the dif-
fusive work of our public libraries has
been animated in late years. It is because I honor so highly the conscience
that has been awakened in the work of
these libraries, and the power they are
acquiring among the institutions of democracy, that I wish to see no waste in
their energies.

VII

SCHOOL–READING

VERSUS

SCHOOL–TEACHING OF HISTORY

SCHOOL–READING

VERSUS

SCHOOL–TEACHING OF HISTORY[1]

IF I did not know the fact to be other-wise, I should suppose that a desire for some satisfying knowledge of the past life of mankind, and especially within the range of direct ancestries and inherit-ances, would be one of the keenest crav-ings of every active mind. That it is not so is too obvious to need proof; and I think that, on reflection, we can under-stand the fact. That which lies near to us and in sunlight will naturally, always, engage our attention more easily and hold it more strongly than that which

[1] Read at a meeting of the Buffalo Historical Society, to which teachers of history were invited, May, 1906.

is shadowed and remote. The bit of re-
cently past time which we call the Present
is our sunlighted portion of time, and
its subjects and objects of interest are
pressed most insistently upon us. To
a great extent we are compelled to give
them the first place in our thoughts;
because our means of subsistence, and
therefore our lives, are dependent on
things and conditions, not as they have
been, but as they are. Our social relations, moreover, our ambitions, our activities of all kinds, are under the same
control. Those things and conditions, to
be sure, have their roots in the past and
their growth out of it; but the fruits that
are ripening from them *now* are what we
have to gather, for the daily provisioning
of daily life, and they busy us so that we
can easily lose thought of the historic
soils and saps from which they came.

It is thus, by a thousand imperative
needs and interests, that the Present, or
what we call so, wins a natural domina-

tion, and may even take the nearly full possession, of our minds. I can understand, therefore, how and why the majority of people feel no apparent want of any knowledge beyond that which the morning newspaper supplies, of men and things in the world of the passing day : the practical knowledge that suffices for traffic, speculation, partisan politics, social conversation, and other immediate interests in life. I can understand, too, how and why it is that so many, among the people whose appetite of the brain calls for meats which the reporters of the daily press cannot serve to them, prefer other kinds of knowledge before that of human history, caring more to know how the earth got its structure, or how beasts, birds, and insects acquired their variations, or how plants are best classified, or how the forces in nature are related to each other, than to know something of the experience that the generations of mankind have gone through, in their long procession down the ages of the dead; something of the influences that have played upon them, — the changes in outward circumstance and inward state that they have undergone, — the successions of their tasks, their achievements, their struggles, — out of which have come Humanity as we know it, Life as we live it, Society as we make part of it, the Earth as we, the latest heirs to that human-family estate, find it fitted and furnished for our habitation. I can see all such preference of Science before History to be natural, because it is consequent on the overpowering pressure with which present objects and present interests are forced upon the attention of our minds. Science in general is a study for the most part of things as the student sees them with his own eyes, — the phenomena of his own day, — and it tends, as commerce and society and newspapers do, to cultivate habits of mental seclusion within some limited region of passing time. There is no fault to be found with the preference of that study, choosing the good knowledge of Science before the good knowledge of History; nor need we blame the more practical choice which rates a necessary knowledge of the existing conditions of life above the interesting knowledge of how those conditions came to be what they are. There is no fault, I say, to be found with such preferences, except where they put History quite out of consideration, as they often seem to do. That goes beyond my understanding; for it is no natural consequence of anything that the obtrusive and exacting Present imposes upon us.

In saying that the prevalent disposition to put History behind other more obtrusive matters of knowledge is natural and explainable, I do not mean to imply that it is reasonable, or that Science is of more importance than History, or that the Present holds more of the valuables of life than are stored for us in the remembered Past. There are no such comparisons to be made. Present and Past, from the same spinning of time, into the same never-broken thread, woven into the same continuous fabric of human life, have no divisible value to us. Neither can *be* to us nor signify to us anything independently of the other. The Past has its explanations in the Present, the Present in the Past. Whatever real substance of knowledge we get into our minds, and whatever real substance of satisfaction we get into our lives, must come from both.

Mr. Rhodes, the historian, in an excellent address which he made on taking the chair of the presidency of the American Historical Association, in 1899, conceded too much, I think, on this point. " The Present," he said, " is more important than the Past, and those sciences which contribute to our comfort, place within reach of the laborer and mechanic as

common necessaries what would have
been the highest luxury to the Roman
emperor or to the king of the Middle
Ages, contribute to health and the pre-
servation of life, and, by the development of railroads, make possible such
a gathering as this, — these agencies, we
cheerfully admit, outrank our modest
enterprise, which, in the words of Herodotus, is 'to preserve the remembrance of
what men have done.' " I cannot agree
with this view. I would say, on the contrary, that History has an underlying and
upholding relation to every science and
every industry, and cannot, therefore, be
outranked by any. We could not even
choose our foods for to-day's dinner if
we had nothing from the Past of mankind
to instruct us concerning the gifts of
nature that are eatable and those that
are not. That is History, on its simplest
side. No man of to-day could even form
the conception of a railroad locomotive,
and far less construct one, if History had

not brought to him the ideas of Watt and Stephenson from a century ago. It is so with everything in the passing day that we do or wish to do, that we obtain or wish to obtain, that we know or wish to know : there is something of History behind it all which we *must* understand if the doing or obtaining or knowing is to be a possible thing.

And it is not alone in those outward ways that the Past comes historically into every present moment. It has more entrance than we are apt to suspect into all the chambers and all the processes of our minds. We do no thinking, we exercise no imagination, we have no emotion, without it. For what is memory but the private historical collection which each man makes for himself? It may be limited very closely to the annals of his own life, — to the little region of his own doings and experiences ; but even at the narrowest, there will always be something from a larger history that has crept into it, and which has some kind of vague participation in his feelings and thoughts. Names, at least, that carry some historical meaning, will have got a lodgment in his brain. Washington, Shakspere, Columbus, Cæsar, Marathon, Magna Charta, the Declaration of Independence, the French Revolution, and other men, movements, and documents of the Past, *will* figure, in some dim way, in his beliefs, and in the general notions that run through all the workings of his mind. Try to conceive, if you can, the state of a human consciousness in which absolutely nothing of such historical idea-stuff is contained; then, perhaps, you can realize how much the more or less of it has to do with the measure and quality of our lives. The historical memory, in fact, is like an atmosphere in our mental world, making it spatial, putting distance, perspective, scenery into it, by refractions and diffusions of our consciousness, which otherwise would be like the flash on flash of straight sun-rays to an eye looking out from the airless moon, which could never see aught but the sun itself. Without its importation of something from the long Past into the sensations of the momentary present, our lives would be like the journey of a traveler through dark tunnels underground.

To think of this is to recognize the absolute emptiness of those current instants of time which we call the Present, except as we bring furniture to them by importation from the Past, in private stores that are Memory or in public stores that are History. We not only borrow from the days that are gone every power that enables us to extort the practical necessities of life from this present day, but we go to them for everything that lends interest to the passing days of our lives. This is the great fact which puts historical knowledge, in my esteem, above all other matters of knowledge that man can seek. By enrichment

of his consciousness it enriches everything that is interesting in his life. The
realm of his mind is narrow or large in
its resources of interest, according to the
radius of its historical horizon and its
scenic vision of general human life. Historical knowledge is needed, therefore,
for all minds, as the indispensable furniture of a satisfying mental life. The man
of science and the man of business can
give room to it, not only with no detriment
to the specialized occupations of their
thought, but with gains of animation and
enlargement that could come, I am sure,
from nothing else. It is the one kind of
knowledge which, more than any other,
is expansive in its whole effect; which
resists the monotonizing of interests
and the narrowing of views. "Histories," says Bacon, in his pregnant essay
on "Studies," — "histories make men
wise," and he gave them the first place
in all that he commends.

These, to me, are the all-sufficient

reasons for an early and long and large use of History in educational work. The more specific pleas for it, urged commonly: that it exercises the judgment and the imagination, — that it is full of ethical lessons and instructive examples of character, — that it will cultivate pa- triotism, and the like, — are not so strong. They are all true; there is sound argu- ment in them all; but they are all tran- scended by the fact that, in the nature of the human mind, its very capacity for any knowledge, and its pleasure in any, are dependent on the spatial and per- spective conditions imparted to it by its own historian, the Memory. More or less of History it must carry among its con- tents, in order to be at all an intelligent mind. For its richest and best endow- ment of power to do and to enjoy, in any field of human endeavor, it cannot be freighted with too much.

What, then, can be more important in education than the use of means and

efforts to overcome those strenuous pres-
sures and influences which tend naturally
to hold the attention of people too closely
to things of the passing day, blinding
them to the wonderful landscapes of the
historic Past, and depriving them of its
immeasurable enrichment of the life of
the mind? Until recent years History
had no well-recognized place in common
or general schemes of education. Now
it is winning a fairly acknowledged foot-
ing in our elementary and secondary
schools, but only by hard contention and
competition with studies that offer, as it
seems to me, no comparable gifts of culture or power. The claims for it are still
too low. Its place should not be in the
ruck of an overcrowded curriculum, but
clear in the van of preferred subjects,
through all grades from the middle, at
least, of every elementary course. I venture to predict that the consideration it
is beginning to receive will soon give it
an unquestioned title to that place. Fur-

thermore, I shall venture to submit some speculations of thought that I have indulged myself in, concerning a school treatment of History which might possibly be more effectual than the modes of treatment now pursued. I am not a teacher; I have done no teaching at any time of my life; and I should be guilty of great presumption if I spoke with dogmatism on the subject; but I think there can be no impropriety in a plain statement of my thought to those who can give it consideration from the teacher's point of view.

I assume that the general purpose and aim of the work done in our school-rooms is not to stock the minds of the young with a provision of knowledge, in any department, that will suffice them for their lives; but rather to introduce them to knowledge, — prepare them to be receptive of it, — acquaint them with its attractions and its uses, —put them in the way of pursuing the acquisition of it through later life, and familiarize them with the paths of that pursuit. This must be so in the matter of History, if in nothing else. No intelligent teachers of History will think that they have given as much of it to their classes as can be for the pupils' good. On the other hand, no teachers will work with an eye to the turning out of whole classes of professional historians, trained for exhaustive research, and destined to devote their lives to the study and original construction of history from its sources in public and private depositories of important fact. For one in a thousand, perhaps, the instruction fitted to that end might be given profitably; but it would not be of profit to the remaining nine hundred and ninety-nine. The service of the school to them in this matter must simply be such as to make them lovers of the literature of History, — lovers, that is, of History as a finished product of trained research and judgment and literary art. In a word,

I would say that the office of the school in its educational use of History is to evoke the appetite for historical reading, and to prepare judgment and taste for a right choice of writers and books.

Is this office performed in the best possible way by any method of teaching History now employed in our schools? I have been led to serious doubts on that point; and my doubts have gone so far as to question whether the results I have indicated *can* be attained satisfactorily by any treatment of History that would be describable as "teaching," in the customary use of the word. I have read many excellent papers on such methods, written by wise and earnest teachers, of great experience; and the fine thought and spirit in most of them have impressed me very much; but at the base of them all, I find more or less of a catechising requirement which cannot, as I would judge, be favorable to the reading-interest and habit that we wish to create. It involves a piece-meal treatment of the details in an historical narrative, which breaks the continuity of impression from them on the pupil's mind. But most of that allured and prolonged attention which we call "interest" depends on this very continuity of impressions which such treatment breaks up. For History is, essentially, a story, and my feeling is that it must not be spoiled *as* a story by anything done to it in the schools. Whatever it carries, of political, moral, and other meanings and teachings, is carried in the current of its story, not, I am sure, to be fished out with question-hooks, but to be borne fluently into the mind, with the stream, which will create for it a welcoming thirst.

What I wish to argue for, therefore, is the simple *reading* of History in schools, with no analytical teaching, questioning, or periodical examination, to break the thread of the tale which the school or the class pursues. Of course it should be systematic reading, under the lead of a capable teacher, whose accompanying comments may emphasize, explain, illuminate, and illustrate, here and there, according to need ; but, as nearly as possible, it ought, I think, to preserve the effect which a mind experiences in taking information to itself, by its own volition and its own absorption, from a printed page. Leave the matter of the reading to have what fate it will in various minds ! Trust all immediate results to the ultimate result ! What if the daily leakage from young minds is large, provided we are opening inlets to them from springs in later years that will never run dry ! Let us remember the stream-likeness of this story of the Past, and allow it to trickle its course through such irrigating brain-channels as it finds, with no incessant casting of lead-lines to test its depth ! It is not in this matter as it is with the little cisterns of Arithmetic and Grammar and Geography that we try to fill, once for all, in the brain. There the quizzing plummet and the examination dredge have their proper use. Here we are introducing something very different, for a very different action and agency; something to be for a general diffusion, expansion, refreshment, and stimulation of all consciousness, all feeling, all imagination, all thought. Then why not give it free play, meddling as little as possible with its natural flow and with the natural deposits it will leave?

In my thought of this treatment of History, in elementary and secondary schools, the scheme of it would be something like this:

1. An underlying use of such readable text-books of abbreviated History as can be found; such text-books as are not mere packages of assorted fact, but which give a fluent showing of the main movements of events, with a moderate amount of detail. These to be carriers, as it were, of the historical narrative through its

less important parts, where they suffice to keep interest alive or to make the connection with coming incidents understood.

2. The bringing in of passages and chapters from the classic and standard works of historical literature at all points in the narrative where a broader and more vivid treatment can be introduced with marked effect.

3. A judicious accompaniment of comment and explanation by the directing teacher, restrained carefully to avoid much diversion of mind from the reading itself.

For example, if I planned an experiment in this treatment of History with a class of young people, I would take such a book as might easily be made out of Freeman's "General Sketch of European History" and use it for the threading of careful selections from the best historical literature within its field. It is a book that needs revision of its first two chapters,

to bring into it later views and revelations
in ethnology and Greek archæology;
otherwise it seems to me to be excellent
in its adaptation to such a use. It could
introduce bits of reading, in the first instance, from the Iliad and from some of
the Greek hero-myths, in connection with
extracts from popular accounts of the
explorations at Troy, Mycenæ, and in
Crete, which throw light on their sources
in historical fact. For a first reading in
Greek history, Freeman's sketch gives
enough of the origin and general course
of the Persian wars; but the stories of
Marathon, Thermopylæ, and Salamis
should be read in Herodotus, or in
Plutarch's Miltiades or Themistocles,
or in both. Then I would carry the reading to those short sections of the first
book of Thucydides (89 to 99) in which
he tells in his plain way " how the Athe-
nians attained the positions in which they
rose to greatness " after the destruction
of their city in the last of the Persian

wars; how they formed the Confederacy
of Delos and took the leadership of it;
how they abused their domination, made
subjects of their allies, and so aroused
the hostilities and jealousies that brought
ruin upon them in the ensuing Peloponnesian War. To this I would add the
later part of Plutarch's life of Aristides,
which tells of the strengthening of democracy at Athens at the end of the Persian wars and gives further particulars
of the formation of the Delian Confederacy; and I would draw yet more from
Plutarch by liberal extracts from his lives
of Themistocles and Pericles. To deepen
and widen the impression from this, the
great period in Greek history, I know of
nothing better to be brought to a young
class than may be found in chapters XVI
and XVII of Evelyn Abbott's book on
"Pericles and the Golden Age of Athens."
I am not sure that Freeman's slight
sketch of the Peloponnesian War would
need any enlargement; but something

from Thucydides and Xenophon, and from Plutarch's Alcibiades and Lysander, might supplement it interestingly and with profit. As for the period between the Peloponnesian War and the intrusion of Philip of Macedon into Greek affairs, there seems to be little call for going beyond Freeman's brief account.

On coming to the Macedonian epoch it would undoubtedly be desirable to interest our young readers somewhat more, not only in the extraordinary conquests of Alexander, but in the preparatory work of Philip, his father, who was the abler and greater man of the two. My suggestion would be to take something in the first instance, for that purpose, from Plutarch's Demosthenes, and a few pages from the 66th and 67th of Niebuhr's "Lectures on Ancient History," where both Philip and his great Athenian opponent are estimated with much fairness of view. Concerning the immeasurable importance of Alexander's heroic career, in its effects upon subsequent history, there is no room for two opinions; but historians have differed so widely in their estimates of the hero that young readers should be acquainted, I think, with the opposing views. Thirlwall admires him and credits him largely with the great results that came from what he did. Grote does not. Perhaps there could be selections from each. After the death of Alexander, I judge that Freeman has told all that can be made interesting or instructive to the average school-boy or school-girl, down to the time when Greek history is merged in that of Rome.

Turning, then, to the latter, I would plan a similar course, in which Freeman should furnish the links of connection between readings from Livy, Plutarch, Polybius, Cæsar, Tacitus, Mommsen, Merivale, Gibbon, and many more.

If half an hour daily could be given to such readings, during seven or eight years of the period spent by a pupil

in graded school and high school, they
would not only carry him, I judge, over
very wide ranges of general history, and
into familiarizing and appetizing touch
with its best literature, but ample time
would remain, I am sure, for repetitions
and enlargements of the more important
parts of the tour. Possibly in such repetitions, traversing English and American
history for the second time, more leisurely
and with more nearly ripened minds,
there might be something of the step-by-
step "teaching" introduced with advantage. It might then be possible to scru-
tinize, analyze, correlate, and otherwise
discuss events and incidents one by one,
without destroying interest in the historical movement to which they belong;
but I cannot believe that a first reading
of history should be broken in any such
way. I cannot believe that a tape-meas-
urement of "lessons" in it, with a halt
for quizzing at each mark on the tape, is
as educational in this matter as a free

excursion would be. I cannot believe that History will waken the feeling that it ought to excite in the mind of a young student, if it is thrust upon him in a dry compend, which he must glue his un-willing eyes to, while remembering al-ways that the trigger of an examination trap may be lurking in every name, date, and circumstance that it holds. For His-tory, if for nothing else that the school gives him, I would ease him of that dread, and make him free to experience pleasure and desire. I would make him his own examiner, by requiring him, at intervals, to write a summary in his own language of what he has gathered from the last week or fortnight of the readings. There is no other process of durable memorizing that equals that ; and I be-lieve it could be trusted, in connection with such readings as I suggest, to yield better results than are coming from the catechized "study" of History now pur-sued in our schools.

I know the hazard of my venture in theorizing without practical experience, and I am prepared to have it shown to me that my suggestions are impracticable, or that, if practicable, they would not answer my expectations in the result. If experience so adjudges them, I only ask to be told why.